End of an Era

DAVID PLOWDEN

End of an Era

The Last of the
Great Lakes Steamboats

New York   W. W. Norton & Company   *London*

The text of this book is composed in Electra.
Composition by Trufont Typographers.
Printed and bound in Great Britain by Balding & Mansell plc.
Book design by Hugh O'Neill.

First Edition.

Library of Congress Cataloging-in-Publication Data

Plowden, David.
The last of the Great Lakes steamboats / by David Plowden.
p.   cm.
ISBN 0-393-03348-1
1. Lake steamers—Great Lakes—History—Pictorial works.
2. Steam navigation—Great Lakes—History—Pictorial works.
I. Title.
VM460.P56   1992
386′.22436—dc20
91-31827
CIP

ISBN 0-393-03348-1

W.W. Norton & Company, Inc.   500 Fifth Avenue, New York, N.Y. 10110
W.W. Norton & Company, Ltd.   10 Coptic Street, London WC1A 1PU

1 2 3 4 5 6 7 8 9 0

DEDICATION
To the memory of my father

ACKNOWLEDGMENTS

It would be impossible for me to acknowledge the many who in one way or another helped me bring this project to fruition. Inevitably I would forget to mention someone who deserves to be thanked. There are so many people that this book would become a veritable "Who's Who" of the lakes. Instead I hope all will realize that I owe a deep debt of gratitude to each and every one of you who generously shared so much of your time and knowledge with me. I hope you will accept a heartfelt collective thank you. Without your interest, advice, and help this book would have been impossible. I enjoyed knowing you and all the time I spent with you during the past few years.

As with every book there are a few people whose contributions were beyond the "call of duty." I would like to give special thanks to James W. Gaskell, president of Inland Lakes Management, Inc., who during the last five years so graciously allowed me access to the vessels in his fleet of venerable steamers; and to Captain Eugene P. Stafford, the company's vice president—Administration, with whom I spent many interesting hours discussing steamboats, and who answered so many of my interminable questions. To Norman R. Martinson, Inland Lakes' vice president—Hull and Machinery, goes a special debt of gratitude for being my expert on all manner of technical matters relating to steam engines, and for sharing with me his great fund of knowledge about lake steamers. Your contributions have been invaluable. I should also not like to forget Elaine Oliver, who must have answered several hundred telephone calls of mine over the course of the past five years asking for the whereabouts of the *S. T. Crapo* and the *E. M. Ford*. My thanks also go to Mr. J. J. Davis, president of the Kinsman Lines, Inc., who so kindly gave me permission to photograph on board his company's vessels so many times during the past five years. To Captain Al Ritteman, retired, former master of the *William A. McGonagle*, thank you for allowing me the run of your ship on so many occasions in Buffalo and Duluth. To Jack Yewell of Oglebay Norton Company, I would like to express my thanks for arranging those trips on board the *J. Burton Ayers* and the *Crispin Oglebay*—and for enabling me to spend what seems to have been the better part of a year on board those two grand old boats. Another special word of thanks goes to Dale W. App, general manager of USS Great Lakes Fleet, for your encouragement and interest in this project, and for allowing me to spend so much time onboard the *Irvin L. Clymer* during her last season. I am glad to have gained a new friend through our mutual love of steamboats, and look forward to continuing our association. To Captain Dietlin, master of the *Clymer* in her last season, who shared with me many of his reminiscences of a lifetime on the lakes. And to Ilona Mason, one of USS's fleet's dispatchers in Duluth; thanks for helping me to keep track of the *Clymer* last year.

A very special word of thanks must go to a few more: To Captain Howard Fisher, Bruce Matthes, Bob Hensley, Steve Habermehl, Leonard Werda, Mark Booth, Rodney Ruell, Joe McKay, and the other officers and crew of the *S. T. Crapo* who have made me feel as if she were a second home, whether in port or out on the lakes. To two others whom I now consider among my friends, Bob Noffze, captain of the *Crispin Oglebay*, and Edward "Bud" Tambourski, captain of the *J. Burton Ayers*, I shall never forget those memorable trips in the summer of 1990, and all the hours I spent on board in ports all over the lakes. To the "chiefs" Jack Fredericks and Brian Krus, and Dick McCarthy, the *Oglebay*'s first assistant engineer, thanks for giving me the run of the engine room, and for all the hours you spent explaining its mysteries. To John Biolchini, first mate on the *Oglebay*, who explained to me so much about ship handling. To Terry Reynolds, second mate on the *Oglebay*, thanks for your lessons in navigation, and Jim Roth, third mate on the *Ayers* showing my family all round the ship that night in Calcite—and for giving my daughter, Karen, your hard hat. A most special word of thanks must go to another new friend, Mike Medvick, assistant cargo manager of Columbia Transportation Division of Oglebay Norton, who arranged all those rendezvous with the *Oglebay* and the *Ayers* over the last few years. I don't know what I would have done without your help. We must have spoken to each other on the telephone at least once a day during this project. I shall miss not having an excuse to pick up the phone and hear your voice saying, "Mike speaking."

My enduring gratitude to all of you. I hope our paths cross again.

In addition I would most especially like to thank Michael J. Dills of the Freshwater Press in Cleveland—author, editor, and one of the great authorities on the Great Lakes—for sharing so much knowledge with me and for helping me avoid making glaring errors. I would also like to thank members and staff of the Great Lakes Historical Society and Museum in Vermilion, Ohio, the Steamboat Historical Society of America, and all the various steamship companies on the lakes who took such trouble in answering my inquiries and for helping me with my research. Lastly I would like to express my gratitude to Dr. Paul Johnstone, curator of Maritime History, and William L. Withuhun, deputy chairman of Science & Technology at the Smithsonian Institution's National Museum of American History, for their encouragement and assistance in getting this project underway. And I would also like to thank Frank O. Braynard for helping me to verify some of the arcane facts of steamboat history.

To Jim Mairs, my editor, and Hugh O'Neill, Norton's art director, many thanks for producing yet another beautiful book. To Cecil Lyon, editorial assistant, who took this project to heart, and did so much to steer it safely to its conclusion. Many thanks for all the hours and care you spent. I enjoyed working with you. Once again my deepest gratitude to my dear, old friend Glenn Hansen for being my right hand in the darkroom and helping me solve all the many photographic problems we encountered—not the least of which was T-Max film!

Finally, I would like to thank my best friend of all, my wife, Sandra, who not only spent an entire summer chasing boats around the Great Lakes with me—all the while keeping our two children, Philip and Karen, who had had their fill of steamboats, occupied—but read and re-read my manuscript, listened to all my tales of woe and joy ad infinitum. As always your love sustained me through thick and thin.

End of an Era

CHAPTER 1

They mark our age
as a race of men;
earth shall not see
such ships as these again.
— John Masefield

"They told me these didn't exist anymore," said Mark Booth, the young third assistant engineer, on the midnight watch.

"The first time I came into the engine room, I said, 'Oh, God no, they never taught you anything about this in school!'"

And why should they? The day of the reciprocating steam engine is over. In fact, the age of steam barely exists anymore, but tonight in the engine room of the old S. T. Crapo, it is alive and well. I am standing on the crank deck watching the Crapo's staunch old triple-expansion engine, drinking in the sounds of another time.

The engine room is stifling. The smell of oil and hot grease permeates everything. It is a cacophony of mechanisms, a labyrinthine world of condensers, cylinders, pipes, and valves—all arranged seemingly without the slightest logic to the uninitiated. The great engine is at center stage. Everything, everywhere is in constant motion, as if all the mechanical apparatuses ever invented had been assembled together in a bewildering arrangement of flailing rods, pistons, rocker arms, cranks, and tons of steel hurtling 'round and 'round. Every working part is bathed in oil, shining, glistening, working in unison with singular purpose.

The pistons and the crossheads are moving relentlessly up and down, the dancing rods, the rolling cranks turning over and over again, perfectly orchestrated, repeating the same pattern with unerring precision and predictability, as if set in perpetual motion by some unseen hand.

Everything worked in perfect harmony: The eccentrics' seemingly demented motion precisely controlled the valves. Those, in turn, with unerring timing, admitted and expelled the steam from the cylinders driving the pistons down and up, back and forth, imparting the energy embodied in the steam itself through the crossheads to the connecting rods, and from the rods to the cranks and the shaft. The engine seemed so self-sufficient that, once set in motion, it would be able to run on in perpetuity, unhindered by human intervention.

How could anything so primitive and simple at the same time be so complex, precise? There was nothing precious, nothing abstract about the engine. Where else, I thought, is such brute force so finely tuned? It was a machine, pure and simple, an expression of mankind's ability to make things do what flesh and muscle alone cannot accomplish. It was big, robust, so unlike today's inventions, where the marvel is in smallness—in miniaturization often so esoteric that one cannot appreciate its miracle, any more than it is possible to see angels dancing on the head of a pin. There was nothing incomprehensible about the Crapo's old engine, nothing hidden from view behind cowlings, as with most machines. You could see how it worked.

Once there, I was mesmerized. Ever since Alpena, Michigan, some twenty hours ago, this staunch old engine had kept the pace, never skipping a single beat. Not just since Alpena, but from that day sixty-five years ago when the first rush of steam filled its cylinders and the great cranks began to turn. This choreography would not be over until the captain rang "finished with engine" at Detroit tonight. For now the engine just kept driving onward, as if it would go on turning forever, in almost liquid, effortless motion, as if to the end of time. Not so. I had to keep reminding myself that in a few more years, perhaps the command "finished with engine" would be rung for the last time, and this hot, vibrant engine would become cold and useless. But tonight, down here below the waterline on the Crapo, the age of steam and coal and the principle that heat equals work are intact and vital, as I always remembered them being.

No matter that I came in from another place where steam engines don't exist. Here was one working away as if oblivious to the fact that its day was done. The engine was the same as a thousand others in the hulls of countless vessels that had steamed across the waters of the world for more than a century. The sense of the engine's authority, its power so compelling—it was impossible to contemplate the fact that one day soon this magnificent, useful machine would suffer the ignominy of being melted down and turned into razor blades.

I could see the young engineer above me, arms crossed, leaning against the desk on the throttle deck watching the engine turning. Each of us was totally absorbed in his own way. The engine was his to run, mine to contemplate. Although the great machine seemed to have a life of its own, I knew that it was beholden to the engineer's hand. He controlled its life's blood, steam. I knew the indicator on the "Chadburn" was at "full ahead," and that massive cranks weighing God-knows-how-many tons turning before me at 80 rpm could be stilled in a moment by his bidding.

All at once I was aware of the presence of Nelson Hawley, the oiler. On every watch, twice an hour, each oiler "does a round," checks every piece of moving machinery in the engine room to see if anything is running hot, or doesn't sound quite right. It's the oiler's responsibility to monitor the temperature of all the engine's moving parts, to make sure that none are overheating.

First begins the ritual of oiling. He watches, drawing on the experience of a lifetime ministering to engines; judges the timing exactly, waits for each part to be in exactly the right place, then fills each cup and receptacle with a drop or two of oil—one here, another there. He is precise, performing his work without a single wasted motion, the sign of a man who has performed a task for so many years that it has become second nature. It took him no more than five minutes to work his way 'round the engine. When done, he put down his oilcan, wiped his hands with a rag, and began the second act of his ritual, "feeling 'round."

He stepped onto a platform under the cylinder block, where he stood for a moment amid the blur of pistons, and crossheads just inches away from his head. Once again he gauged the engine's rhythm. This time, it was not the oilcan's spout he thrust into the flailing machinery, but his own hand. Three times on each side of each crosshead bearing, he slapped the back of his hand as it raced up and down. Then on to the next and the next he went taking its temperature the way a parent feels its child's brow. Then down below to the crank deck he descended, to finish his round. He leaned over as far as he could in the space above the shaft amid the thrashing rods and dropped his arm into position so that once again the back of his hand could slap the bearings on the giant cranks.

Twice an hour this short, little man in overalls, with a flashlight in his back pocket, performs this task with all the finesse of a ballet dancer. One false move or misjudgment would shatter his hand.

"How do you do it?" I asked, brimming with unconcealed admiration.

"Gotta have respect for machinery, but you can't be afraid of it. See that cup there?" he asked, pointing his flashlight in the direction of a flailing crank. "If you get too far over, then your finger gets cut off. First put your hand in there to feel where you are. Just slap it a couple of times. Fellows have lost their hands sometimes. If you don't drink, you can do a good job.

"After you get onto it, it comes natural. I just stay relaxed," he answered, shaking his wrist like a limp rag. Relaxed, I thought, putting my arm in there next to tons of steel revolving at 80 rpm!

"Keep it stiff and it'll get broke," he added, thrusting his hand straight-armed into the space above those immense revolving cranks.

"One thing else. I wear no ring, no watch; might get caught, snap off a finger, or an arm," he said with a hint of a smile.

I noticed that he had all his fingers.

"Can you really tell if they're too hot?" I asked.

"Oh, yes, you can feel the temperature. If she's hot, start giving her more oil right away. You can tell."

Maybe Hawley can, but certainly not the average man.

"It's a good engine, this. A working son-of-a-bitch," he said, revealing just a touch of affection for his charge. I commented on the highly polished brass. He told me that the wipers polish it up every Sunday. Then he was gone, poking around that maze of machinery that fills up every nook and cranny of an engine room.

Later I commented on Hawley's performance to the young engineer. He admitted to me that he had tried to "feel 'round" just once—all engineers are required to know how to do it—and "was damn near killed."

"Wonder how many fires I've cleaned?" asked Rodney Ruell, the *Crapo's* fireman on the eight-to-midnight watch, when he paused to light up a cigarette.

"I've been on the *Crapo* sixteen years. I've always been on steam. Always coal. I started out as a coal passer. I've fired the *E. M. Ford*, the *J. B. Ford*, the *Lewis G. Harriman*. Was on the *E. M.* and the *J. B.* when they were still hand fired, before they were converted to oil burners. The *Crapo* was hand fired, too—a 'hand bomber'—before she was converted. She got Stokers [Dayton Marine Underfeed Stokers] in 1962. There are no more 'hand bombers' left on the lakes. The last was the *Chief Wawatam*, the old car ferry across the straits."

For the last hour, I have been watching Rodney cleaning the fires in the *Crapo's* six furnaces. Like Hawley, he is the last of his kind—firemen who once toiled unseen, deep within the bowels of ships, feeding the furnaces, keeping watch over the boilers that turned water into the force that drove them onward.

Rodney has been firing steamers on the lakes for twenty-two years. When he hired out with Huron Cement Company in 1970, coal burners already were well on the road to extinction. Today the *Crapo* is one of the last boats in the world where men like Rodney are needed.

The firehold is the heart of every coal-burning steamer. It is also a little piece of hell—or at least what I envision as hell. It is almost inconceivable to come upon this Dantesque place at the end of the twentieth century. And well it might be, for in America the *S. T. Crapo's* firehold is unique.

Pulling fires is a primitive, dirty—and essential—task. All coal fires produce ash and clinkers as they burn. Unless these are cleaned off the grates periodically, the firebed becomes so thick that it will choke off the air needed for proper combustion. In order to do the cleaning, the fireman "wings" the fire—rakes the good coals from the top of the fire to one side of the furnace. He then pulls the ashes and clinkers from the other side of the grates out of the furnace and onto the deck plates of the firehold, where they are extinguished with water from a hose. When he is finished with one side, he then "wings" the fire from the other side onto the clean grates.

As antediluvian as the *Crapo*'s firehold may seem today, it is a far cry from the way it was when all steam vessels were hand fired. The sweaty, backbreaking tasks that were the lot of every fireman and his indispensable cohort, the coal passer, have gone the way of the coal burners themselves. Firing the boilers used to be an art, according to Norman Martinson, a man who should know. Martinson, who today is fleet engineer for Inland Lakes Management, started out as a coal passer in 1944.

"Somebody who has not done the job would think that you just throw the coal in any which way. But if you didn't place it right, the boiler would not operate properly."

Despite the arduousness of the task of the old-time fireman, Martinson said that many a man preferred the job to others on the lakers: "They didn't have a boss, just a steam gauge. As long as they were able to do their job, nobody bothered them."

Some years ago, Rodney told me that he lived in England. When he paused for a cigarette and a few swigs of coffee—which he always did after cleaning each furnace—I asked him why a fellow from northern Michigan, who worked on the Great Lakes for nine months of the year, had a London address.

"Got tired of going to California. I went over in 1979, liked it, and stayed."

Then he went back to his labors, and once again this Stygian place was filled with hellfires and smoke.

Joe McKay came on watch at midnight. Like Rodney, he, too, is a veteran of twenty-one years in the firehold. Unlike Rodney, who takes a long time to arrange all his weaponry and then sets about the task methodically, Joe attacks the fires with demonic fury.

A huge fiery clinker—an "alligator"—weighing at least 15 pounds fell on the deck plates, from the number 4 furnace. Joe immediately attacked it with slice bar and water hose as if he were engaged in mortal combat with a dragon. Once having subdued it, he grinned proudly, and he asked me if I wanted it. I replied that I really had no need for such a thing.

After he had finished pulling all six fires, he looked over a pile of clinkers with the eye of a connoisseur. Finally he picked up one that seemed to be of his liking. "I keep them sometimes," he said. "Make sculptures from them. Animals usually. Next time I see you, I'll have one for you."

I asked him how he liked his job.

"I don't, but I like the pay."

Virtually alone today, Joe and Rodney are carrying on the tradition of all before them who stoked the myriad furnaces of our industrial world and, to use the words of the poet William Blake, kept the "glowing Poker reddening fierce."

About a month later, I showed up in the firehold again, and Joe, good to his word, had not one but two little clinker sculptures for me.

"Good for paperweights," he said.

I cannot remember the world without the smell of coal smoke and steam engines.

I was born at the beginning of the end of the age of steam. I saw the steam locomotive reach the apex of its development, only to see it succumb to the internal-combustion engine and disappear from America's rails. I missed the heyday of the steamboat by almost a full generation, yet when I was a boy, steamboats were still as plentiful as bluegills in a millpond. Then a line of coal smoke on the horizon was commonplace, and one could come upon a steamboat in almost any port. Although the diesel was in the ascendancy, it was still possible to feel the throb of an old steam engine pounding away below the decks of many a boat.

By the time I graduated from college in 1955, steam as a viable means of locomotion was an endangered species. Today, thirty-seven years later, it is all but extinct. Almost.

For more than three decades, steam has been relegated to the role of a curiosity on America's railroads. Today it has also vanished from almost every body of water on this continent. All the great fleets of steamboats are gone. With the exception of the recently re-activated *Badger* on Lake Michigan, the venerable *Delta Queen*, and a few seasonal excursion steamers—most notably the *Segwun* on Ontario's Muskoka Lakes, and the *Belle of Louisville* on the Ohio—there are currently no vintage passenger steamers in regular service on any of our rivers and lakes. Even the storied Bob-Lo boats, *Columbia* and *St. Claire* on the Detroit River are gone. They were withdrawn from service at the end of the 1991 season, and are currently laid up inactive. Steam whistles no longer echo through the skyscrapers of New York or in Boston Harbor. Save for the diminutive *Sabino* at the Mystic Seaport Museum, and the *Virginia V* at Seattle, there are no steamers on either Long Island or Puget Sound. There are none at all plying New England's coastal waters, nor on Chesapeake Bay, nor anywhere along the Gulf Coast. Not since the fall of 1988, when the *Princess Marguerite* was retired, have any been in regular service on the West Coast. In fact, there are no steamboats in regular commercial service anywhere in America, except on the Great Lakes and the St. Lawrence River.

Here, some 185 years after Robert Fulton steamed up the Hudson in command of his *North River Steamboat of Clermont*, is to be found our last fleet of steamboats still at work carrying the commerce of the nation. These staunch old lake freighters, and the men who run them, are still doing essentially the same tasks they have always performed.

End of an Era is about a particular group of steamboats—the Great Lakes bulk cargo vessels that were at one time, or still are, coal fired, and ones that with a few notable exceptions were originally powered by expansion reciprocating engines. To me, these are the marks of a true steamboat, traits that characterize it as decidedly a nineteenth-century creation. Coal and the reciprocating engine were, after all, the fundamental elements of the age of steam.

After 1945, with the exception of a few replicas no American vessels were built with expansion engines and no coal burners were built after 1953. I have included here only those vessels built before the mid-1950s. This date marked a major turning point in the evolution of marine architecture. Theretofore, the design of all vessels, to one degree or another, reflected the lineage of their predecessors. Afterwards, a radical departure from tradition produced vessels of an entirely different nature; even when steam powered, their lines had little to do with anything that had been built previously.

Quite obviously, I have not included those recent reconstructions that too often are passed off as being the genuine article. Nor have I included any replicas, or vessels that have been restored—as fine as some may be, such as the incomparable *Segwun*, or the sternwheeler *Natchez* on the Mississippi. I also haven't included the brand new and monstrous *Mississippi Queen*. Although she is powered by a vintage Steam engine, and is the largest vessel ever built for service on the Mississippi, her appearance violates every canon of authenticity.

The boats and the men in this book belong to a time whose heyday was not so long ago but already is ancient history when reckoned in American terms. While it may in fact be the final documentation of working steamboats in America, it was never my intention to produce a catalogue of boat profiles, nor was this work to be viewed as comprehensive. Just as a lone Victorian house on a street of used-car lots gives little idea of what a town was like a century ago, it would be folly today to attempt to re-create the heyday of the steamboats.

Virtually the entire fleet of magnificent excursion steamers in North America has been scrapped. Europe, on the other hand, still has a slew of *Dampfschiffe*. A flotilla of assorted, diminutive sidewheelers continues to ply the rivers and lakes of Switzerland, Sweden, Germany, and much of the rest of the continent. Most of these are, indeed, the genuine item, albeit museum pieces. These meticulously restored and maintained pleasure craft include such ancient denizens as the 138-year-old *Skiblandner*, on Norway's Lake Mjøsa—no doubt the oldest steam vessel in service anywhere.

Our last fleet of steamboats is nothing like Europe's, or those Mississippi River sidewheelers depicted belching fire from their stacks in Currier & Ives prints. Nor do they skim through the water like the sleek, flag-bedecked paddlewheelers of the Hudson River Day Line. Unlike the splendidly appointed overnight packets that once called at every port from Boston to Seattle, they have no magnificently carved staircases or dining rooms with tables laid with heavy damask napery. They are nothing like the illustrious transatlantic liners of my parents' and grandparents' time, the *Mauretania* or the *Normandie*; their counterparts on the Great Lakes, the *Keewatin* and *Assiniboia*; or those elegant sisters, *Greater Buffalo* and *Greater Detroit*.

This fleet carries no passengers. Its vessels are not steamboats in the traditional sense, being more akin to oceangoing steamers than those usually associated with our inland waterways. At first sight, they appear to be a cross between a tanker and a freighter. They are mostly hull—huge and plain. Simply put, they are the most prosaic of vessels, neither fancy nor elegant, but workaday steamers that, year in and year out, have performed yeoman service without accolades of any sort. Their stock-in-trade is iron ore, coal, cement, salt, limestone, grain—elemental materials upon which an economic empire was founded, but hardly the most glamorous of cargoes. They are denizens of the industrial world, and as such have never been in the public eye. Their haunts are places like steel mills, grain elevators, coal piers, cement plants, and ore docks. Nonetheless, they have a magisterial bearing like few other vessels have today. They have "line," as the captain of one of them said to me.

The lake steamers in this book are a remarkable fraternity indeed. Among their ranks is reputedly the oldest steam vessel in commercial service in the world. One is our last coal-burning freighter. A handful are still powered by reciprocating engines, a type of marine engine that has all but disappeared as a viable means of propulsion. One of these is quite possibly the only quadruple-expansion engine in service. Another is, as far as known, the sole remaining example of the rare Lenz Standard Marine Engine. Among their ranks are the last steamboats in America with great tall stacks, the last with counter sterns and with hull plates made of solid carbon steel held together by rivets—all hallmarks of an era of steamship design that has vanished almost everywhere else.

So by fate, or chance, or sheer endurance, these old lake freighters have earned a distinction few boats anywhere can claim. Certainly in North America they are without peer. Their distinction lies in the fact that they have survived unchanged from another time—which, although not so long ago, already seems like ancient history.

The fact that fame came late in their careers after years of relative obscurity does not mean they have not earned a place in the pantheon of steamboats. Quite the contrary. Having outlived virtually every vessel of their vintage in North America, they are among the last examples of nineteenth-century marine technology in the Western Hemisphere. This alone gives them a distinction beyond that of most vessels.

They have survived this long primarily because fresh water is kinder to metal than salt water. Whereas the average age of an oceangoing vessel is approximately twenty-five years, boats of twice that age are commonplace on the lakes. There are other factors, too. As a rule, lakeboats are in service only nine months of the year, which means there is ample time during the winter lay-up to make repairs and, where advisable, conversions to more efficient types of machinery. This has often enabled shipowners to uphold higher standards of maintenance and keep older vessels operating far longer than might otherwise be possible. Another reason for their longevity is that these old lakers have been in the business of hauling bulk cargo, a trade in which speed is not of paramount importance. Under the circumstances, the ten, twelve, or fifteen miles per hour provided by a tried-and-true expansion reciprocating steam engine has been adequate.

Moreover, these old engines were stout and rugged machines that could be repaired and kept running with a minimum of investment in time and money. Over the years, they often proved to be more reliable and easier to maintain than the somewhat finickier turbines and diesels. The difference between a reciprocating engine and the others was described to me by an old steamboatman—who should know—as the difference between "a Ford and a racing car." But parts for these old engines are ever harder to come by. When something breaks, its replacement often has to be made to order at great expense. Sometimes parts can be cannibalized from another vessel, but today most of those with the same vintage machinery have been scrapped.

Equally important is the reality that with each year there are fewer and fewer steamboatmen who know how to keep the old engines going.

"It's going to be a lost art," said the fleet engineer of one of the boat companies. "You had to be raised to it."

An old adage runs, "Science owes more to the steam engine than the steam engine owes to science." In many ways, it is true that the engine was the product of "untutored genius," being more mechanical in nature than scientific. While such a premise may be debatable, it was practical men, such as Thomas Savery, Thomas Newcomen, and James Watt, not men of science, who first built steam engines and put them to work. The theory of thermodynamics that made them work was explored well after steam engines had been put to use.

From today's perspective, in an age of electronics and microchips, where scientific and technological tours de force are commonplace, it is hard to realize that something as seemingly primitive as the steam engine was one of the most significant forces in the development of western civilization. Yet, by the middle of the nineteenth century, steam power had become synonymous with progress and was well on its way to transforming the world.

Beginning early on in the century, the "gospel of steam" was extolled by writers and poets alike. "There cannot be a more beautiful and striking exemplification of the union of science and art than is exhibited in the steam engine," said one of its earliest admirers, Benjamin Heywood, the chairman of the Manchester Mechanics Institute in 1825. Perhaps none expressed it as fervently as Kipling in "M'Andrew's Hymn":

Lord, thou hast made this world below the shadow of a dream,
An', taught by time, I tak' it so—exceptin' always Steam.
From coupler-flange to spindle guide I see Thy Hand, O God—
Predestination in the stride o' yon connectin' rod.
John Calvin might ha' forged the same—enormous,
    certain slow—
Ay, wrought in it the furnace flame—*my* "Institutio."

But steam, as with nuclear power today, was not without its detractors. While the majority believed that steam and the benefits of mechanization would finally liberate mankind from our age-old drudgery, many felt it would be our ruination—that people themselves would become machines. Charles Dickens wrote after his first encounter with one, "The piston of the steam engine worked monstrously up and down like the head of an elephant in a state of melancholy madness."

Nonetheless, as long as mankind was dependent on wind and water, the limits of his own physical endurance and the strength of beasts of burden—upon which society had relied from the beginning of civilization—conquest of the material world was beyond his grasp. It wasn't until the discovery and development of steam power at the beginning of the eighteenth century that society finally had at hand the means to bring about this revolution. The harnessing of steam set in motion the process of scientific and technological advances that have been the distinguishing characteristics of the industrial age and have set it apart from all others.

As with all invention, the initial achievements exist for the most part in principle only—save in museums. In reality, they undergo so many modifications and are adapted to fit so many different conditions that their physical appearance and everyday operation bear little resemblance to the prototype. Nowhere is this more true than with the development of the steam engine. The idea of harnessing the power of steam has its roots far back in antiquity. Hero of Alexandria, who devised a rudimentary form of turbine around A.D. 60, was the first to harness the power of vaporized water. However, it was some seventeen hundred years before a practical application of steam power was devised, when it was put to use as a means of pumping water from the depths of coal mines in England. Although the Scottish engineer James Watt traditionally has been called the father of the steam engine, it was an Englishman, Thomas Savery, who received the first patent in 1698. It wasn't until 1712 that the world's first successful piston-operated steam engine was built. This honor belongs to another Englishman, Thomas Newcomen. Nonetheless, Watt's role in world events is assured. In 1769 he took Newcomen's engine and added a condenser, among other refinements, to make it viable from a mechanical and economic point of view. Even before his death in 1819, Watt's contributions had set in motion the chain of events that forever changed the course of civilization.

The name of the person who devised the idea of putting a steam engine in a boat has long been a matter of historical controversy. The earliest recorded use appears to have occurred in the middle of the sixteenth century, when one Blasco de Gary, a Spaniard, maneuvered a small vessel around the harbor in Barcelona. However, it wasn't until the eighteenth century that the idea began to be taken seriously, and there were a number of unsuccessful attempts on both sides of the Atlantic. According to most sources, the first vessel in America to be moved by steam power was built in 1787 by John Fitch, generally credited as the "father of the American steamboat." There were others—such as James Rumsey, Samuel Morey, Oliver Evans, and John Stevens—who were fascinated with the concept of steam propulsion and experimented with ways of adapting it to the maritime world, none of which were a practical success. The honor of being

the world's first steamboat to be used commercially belongs to the *Charlotte Dundas*, which was designed and built by William Symington on the River Clyde in Scotland in 1802.

It was Robert Fulton who may justifiably lay claim to have operated the world's first commercially *successful* steamboat, when on August 17, 1807, his *North River Steamboat of Clermont* set forth up the Hudson. The *Clermont* (as it is incorrectly called) was powered by an engine built by none other than the British firm of Boulton & Watt, for at the time there were no works in America capable of building a reliable steam engine. Although Fulton relied on the contributions of many, his genius, like that of so many innovators, lay in the fact that he was able to put all the elements together so that they worked.

The earliest steamboats were paddlewheelers operating on protected waterways such as harbors and rivers, where there were none of the problems later encountered when the vessels were subjected to the effects of "wave and swell." Nearly a decade was to pass after Fulton's success before steamboats were tried out on the world's oceans and lakes.

Steam made its appearance on the Great Lakes three years before it was used on the North Atlantic. Although there is some controversy about *exactly* which vessel first brought steam to the lakes, it appears that the *Ontario*, launched at Ogdensburg, New York, in April 1817, may have the best claim. The vessel was not a success, however, for it had great difficulty coping with Lake Ontario's seas.

Most historians agree that from a mechanical and commercially successful point of view, the age of steam on the Great Lakes began with the *Walk-in-the-Water*. She was launched on May 28, 1818, on Scajaguada Creek in Black Rock, New York, just above Buffalo. She made her first trip on August 20 and thereafter provided regular service between lake ports. Her promising career was caught short, however, when she was wrecked off Point Abino on Lake Erie in a gale on November 1, 1821.

The first vessel to use steam on a transatlantic crossing was the *Savannah*, which set out from its namesake port bound for Liverpool on May 22, 1819. Like the *Walk-in-the-Water*, the *Savannah* had the appearance of a sailing vessel fashioned with sidewheels. In fact, its diminutive, 90-horsepower engines were used for only 105 hours during that voyage of twenty-seven days. It would be fully twenty years before the world would believe in the ability of steam—enough to trust it as the sole means of powering vessels on the great and open waters of the world.

After the introduction of the steam engine, the submerged screw propeller was a quantum leap in marine engineering. Previously, the only way of propelling steam-driven vessels through the water was by means of paddlewheels—rotating wheels powered by the engine, to which paddles or blades were attached. The term *paddlewheeler* correctly applies only to vessels whose wheels were placed at the side; the term *sternwheeler* applies only to those that were propelled by a single wheel mounted in a frame at the stern.

Paddlewheels were ideally suited for vessels plying shallow waters, and where great maneuverability was of paramount importance, but they were singularly unsuited to coping with heavy weather on open water, where they exhibited a most unfortunate trait: Whenever the vessel rolled in heavy seas, the wheel on one side would be lifted out of the water, while the other would be thrust deep into the water, creating an enormous strain on the engine. Thus, the need for a deeply submerged means of propulsion became of paramount importance if the advantages of steam power were to translate into commercial success on the wide and deep waters of the world. None of the great ocean liners, no dreadnought or "laker," would have been possible without the propeller.

The Swedish-American inventor John Ericsson generally is credited with developing the screw propeller; however, three other men were instrumental: the Frenchman Frédéric Sauvage and the Englishmen Robert Wilson and Francis Pettit Smith. Both Ericsson and Smith, who were unaware of the other's research, received patents for their respective types of propellers within six weeks of each other in the spring of 1836. The first successful application of the new invention came the following year with the aptly named vessel *Archimedes*. (The Greek mathematician's invention, known as the Archimedes screw, was the basis for the development of the propeller.) The maritime world was quick to embrace the new invention, and by midcentury it was well established as the most efficient means of propulsion.

The propeller made its debut on the Great Lakes in 1841 with the launching of the sloop-rigged *Vandalia*, at Oswego, New York. Here, as on the high seas, it quickly proved invaluable, and soon ushered in a new era of lakeboat design.

By 1850, the steam engine in its various forms came to serve mankind's every waterborne need. Just as the locomotive was to replace the beast of burden on land, the steam engine at a stroke freed mankind from a dependence on sail, and the whims of tide and wind. It allowed vessels to steam upstream as easily as downstream, heretofore an impossibility on most of the world's rivers. It is not surprising that in North America—with its vast spaces and plethora of navigable rivers—steam navigation preceded steam locomotion. Although the railroad has always been considered the most important element in determining the development of the American continent, steamboats came first—and steamboats

are still working in regular service today.

Whether demented elephant or beautiful child of art and science, the steam engine was the first mechanism that converted heat energy into mechanical energy. All steam engines, regardless of their type, work on the principle that when water is converted into steam, it *expands*. Initially, all steam engines were reciprocating—in which a piston moves back and forth within a cylinder—hence the name. The piston's linear motion is transmitted by a connecting rod to a crankshaft, which transforms it into rotary motion—rather like a giant bicycle. The steam is admitted and exhausted through valves alternately at either end of the cylinder, thus pushing the piston back and forth and making each stroke a power stroke. For all practical purposes, this makes each cylinder two cylinders. In vessels with a propeller, the engine is installed vertically so the pistons move up and down directly above the shaft.

With few exceptions, reciprocating engines on most modern steam vessels are of the compound, or expansion, type, wherein the steam works successively in two or more cylinders, rather than in only one, thus increasing the efficiency of the engine considerably. As steam decreases in pressure, it expands, so each successive cylinder in the sequence must be larger than the one before it. For years, the most commonly used marine steam engine was the triple-expansion engine, in which the steam passes through a high-pressure cylinder, an intermediate cylinder, and finally a low-pressure cylinder.

The principle of compounding was developed by one of Watt's contemporaries, Jonathan Hornblower, who patented such an engine in 1781. However, it would be almost a century before boilers were capable of generating the high steam pressure essential to the practical operation of expansion engines.

On virtually all vessels powered by steam engines, the steam is exhausted into a condenser, where it is reconverted into water. On saltwater ships, this condensate is returned to the boiler, where it becomes steam once again in a never-ending cycle. On most freshwater vessels, where there is no need to use the condensate, it is discharged over the side. The condensing process also creates a vacuum, which enables the steam in the low-pressure cylinder to work at a relatively higher pressure. The greater the vacuum, the greater the efficiency of the engine.

The dimensions of the cylinders determined not only the horsepower of the engine but ultimately its practical size. As ever-larger engines were built, the diameters of the cylinders increased proportionally, finally reaching the point where the low-pressure cylinder was simply too large and too heavy to use. This problem could be overcome in a "triple" by dividing the low-pressure cylinder in half, thus creating a four-crank triple-expansion engine that provided additional horsepower without the disadvantages of an elephantine low-pressure cylinder.

The quadruple-expansion engine—a "triple" with a second intermediate cylinder through which the steam passes en route to the low-pressure cylinder—was essentially a creature of the late nineteenth century, being in general use only from about the 1890s to 1910. Ironically, the "quad," which was designed to power the largest vessels of the day, proved to be a brontosaurus. As ships continued to increase in size, so did the need for ever-more-powerful engines. The immense size of the "quad" proved to be its undoing. The additional power and speed it produced proved to be insignificant compared to its great weight. The triple, especially in its four-cylinder form, was proven to be inherently a far more efficient engine.

At the apex of their development, in the years prior to World War I, multi-expansion engines were used to power the largest battleships and the fastest express liners of the day. Because of their immense size, these engines often were referred to as "cathedrals of metal"—an apt description, considering the fact that these towering vertical machines stood several decks high and were held in place by huge steel columns not unlike the buttresses of a cathedral.

It was in German hands that this engine reached its zenith. The Hamburg-American Line's steamer *Deutschland*, launched in 1900, sported twin quadruple-expansion engines of 17,000 horsepower each. Its rival, North German Lloyd's *Kaiser Wilhelm II*, built three years later, had what probably were the most powerful engines of this type ever built: two pairs of two complete quadruple elements arranged in tandem, each of which produced some 20,000 horsepower. The monstrous low-pressure cylinders were 9 feet 4 inches in diameter, something of a record for marine engines.

The triple-expansion engine appears to have reached its apogee in 1893, with the British Cunard liners *Campania* and *Lucania*. These two sisters were powered with two 15,000-horsepower, five-cylinder, triple-crank behemoths—which, as far as I know, were the largest engines of this kind ever built.

The last of the giant triples were used to power many of the world's largest naval vessels. Among these were what were perhaps the most powerful reciprocating marine engines ever constructed in this country: those installed in a trio of U.S. battleships—*New York*, *Oklahoma*, and *Texas*—which were launched between 1912 and 1914. Each of these vessels had a pair of 14,500-horsepower, four-cylinder triples, which produced a prodigious 29,000 horsepower.

The triple made its debut on the Great Lakes in 1888, with the steamer *Cambria*, and proved ideally suited to the slow-paced lake freighter. Soon it became the most widely used engine for this class of vessel, and it was to remain the standard means of propulsion on the lakes long after it fell into disuse elsewhere. Very few quads were built for service on the Great Lakes, where speed—which required engines of great horsepower—was never a primary consideration. An exception were the so-called college boats—bulk carriers such as the *Cornell*, *Harvard*, and *Princeton*—which were built for the Carnegie interests in 1900. Despite the fact that so few were built, it is ironic, indeed, that the oldest steamboat on the lakes today, the *E. M. Ford*, is powered by a quad built in 1897. In all probability, it is not only the last of its kind, but also the oldest marine steam engine in regular commercial service anywhere in the world.

Perhaps the most renowned triple of all was the one built during World War II for the famous Liberty ships, which powered more vessels than any other engine. Although the exact number is not known, some 3,300 of these 2,500-horsepower engines were built on both sides of the Atlantic between 1940 and 1945.

Although turbines were used extensively by then, even on cargo vessels of comparable size, the choice of a triple-expansion engine was not as illogical as it might first seem. This was an emergency, where the need was paramount to produce ships as rapidly as possible. Furthermore, these vessels were to be used in convoy service, where speeds of only 11 knots were necessary. The reciprocating engine was a simple, staunch, reliable machine that could be built by many a shop unfamiliar with marine engines. It needed none of the sophisticated machining required in the construction of turbines.

At the same time as the Liberty ships were being built, the U.S. Maritime Commission authorized construction of sixteen bulk freighters—to help transport the increased wartime tonnage on the Great Lakes. In a sense, these vessels may be said to have been the Great Lakes equivalent of the Liberties. These Maritime-class vessels, launched in 1943, were the last ones built with expansion reciprocating engines on the lakes. Whereas only two of the 2,708 Liberties are known to have survived—the *Jeremiah O'Brien*, which is docked in San Francisco as a memorial to its class and the former schoolship, *John W. Brown*, recently rebuilt at Baltimore—there are still five operational Maritime-class boats on the Great Lakes. Two of these are still powered by their original triples.

With the launching of the last of the Liberties in June 1945, the era of the triple was at an end. With the exception of a comparatively few built with unaflow engines, all commercial steam vessels constructed thereafter were propelled by turbines.

During the years prior to World War I, the reciprocating

expansion engine reached its practical limits of size and speed. By then it had been used universally for almost every marine steam engine over 300 horsepower, with the exception of certain types of paddlewheel vessels and smaller craft, such as harbor tugs. But a new era was at hand. The steam turbine had already made its debut. It was destined to revolutionize marine engineering as the engine of choice for the new breed of large ocean liners and warships. Its great advantage is its ability to create tremendous horsepower in a comparatively small space. Nonetheless, the reciprocating engine was inherently more reliable than the turbine—and far simpler to maintain. Because of its dependability and durability, the triple continued to be used—albeit in ever-diminishing numbers—to power merchant vessels of moderate and small size the world over for many years.

The steam turbine is a far cry from the old "up-and-down" reciprocating engine. It has none of the drama. Its workings are encased beneath shrouds of metal unseen to the eye. It is a masterpiece of efficiency, though, when compared to the "slam-bangin'" triple—a whirring rotary engine that converts the thermal energy of steam into mechanical energy. This task is accomplished by directing a stream of high-velocity steam against a set of blades mounted on a disk attached to a shaft. To be efficient, turbines must rotate at very high speeds—far greater speeds than those at which a propeller can operate. To compensate, reduction gears are used to lower the shaft speed to the point where the propeller can turn at its optimal speed.

While the principle of the turbine is simplicity itself, it is in fact a highly sophisticated and complicated machine. It has many variations, including several compound forms where, just as in its reciprocating counterparts, the same steam is used several times. In some cases, turbines were used to drive electric generators, which were in turn attached to the shaft. These turbo-electrics were deemed not nearly as efficient as the turbine's other forms. They were used primarily in circumstances where a vessel needed large amounts of additional electric power, and they were in general use in the 1930s and early 1940s. However, these engines could produce a prodigious amount of energy, as illustrated by the incomparable French liner *Normandie*, whose four turbo-electric alternators created 160,000 shaft horsepower.

The concept of the turbine has been known since earliest antiquity. Its progenitor—the waterwheel—has been used for centuries. However, it was not until the 1880s that the steam turbine as we know it today was developed by the British engineer Sir Charles Parsons and the Swedish inventor Carl G. P. de Laval. The first vessel in history to use this new engine was the aptly named *Turbinia*, which was unveiled to the world at a celebration marking Queen Victoria's Diamond Jubilee in June 1897. Its then-incredible speed, in excess of 30 knots, so impressed the maritime world that shipowners lost no time in embracing this new form of motive power.

The turbine quickly proved to be far more efficient than the great quads it was destined to replace, where great power and speed were paramount—nowhere more so than with the magnificent British liners *Lusitania* and *Mauretania*, the first large turbine-powered ships, launched in 1906. The power plant of the *Mauretania*, which remained the fastest ship in the world for twenty-two years, produced some 78,000 horsepower, twice that of any ship previously built.

Despite the turbine's great advantage over the expansion engine, several early transatlantic liners were powered by a combination of reciprocating and turbine machinery. Most notable among these were the ill-fated *Titanic* and her sister, the *Olympic*. On these, the two outside propellers were driven by 15,000-horsepower triples, while the center screw was driven by a single turbine placed astern of the reciprocating engines, where it utilized the last of the steam's energy exhausted from the respective low-pressure cylinders.

The reciprocating engine was so well adapted to the Great Lakes trade that the steam turbine did not make an appearance there until 1925, with the Bradley Transportation Line's *T. W. Robinson*—the first large lake steamer so powered. It was propelled with a 3,600-shaft-horsepower General Electric steam-turbo-electric engine, which was minuscule when compared to that of the *Normandie*. It was not until 1938, however, that the first fleet of turbine-driven boats appeared, when the Pittsburgh Steamship Company built four ore carriers equipped with two-cylinder, double-reduction-geared, compound-type de Laval turbines: the *John Hulst*, *William A. Irvin*, *Governor Miller*, and *Ralph H. Watson*.

The turbine was not the last type of steam engine to be developed for marine use. That distinction belongs to a form of reciprocating engine known as the unaflow—"a lovely engine," according to the chief engineer. The unaflow was first patented in America in 1857; contrary to popular belief, it was not a German invention. Although used in two small vessels on Lake Chautauqua in New York, its application was confined largely to stationary engines. The first practical adaptation of these engines for marine use did not come until 1929, when the Skinner Engine Company of Erie, Pennsylvania, built four unaflows to power a quartet of western river towboats.

In all reciprocating engines, including the unaflow, steam enters the cylinders alternately at the top and the bottom of the cylinder. The significant difference between the two is in the method of exhausting steam. In a conventional "up-and-down" engine, part of the steam's energy in one half of the cylinder must be used to expel the used steam from the other half. In the unaflow, the steam is expelled at the end of the power stroke through separate ports "downstroke" from those used by the steam entering the cylinder. The steam always flows in one direction, hence the name *unaflow*. In most engines of this type, high-pressure steam is delivered to all the cylinders. However, there are several types of compound unaflows, including the steeple compound, in which a high- and a low-pressure cylinder are arranged vertically and in tandem.

Because the unaflow has no back pressure, its great advantage from an operational viewpoint was its ability to go from full ahead to full astern "just like that." This made it ideal for such vessels as ferries and harbor tugs, where it was to find its greatest use. Although never used extensively on large vessels, the U.S. Navy chose it to power fifty Casablanca-class escort carriers. Unaflows of several types were used on the Great Lakes, where they were installed in a number of car ferries and several dozen bulk freighters. In fact, the largest unaflow ever built was a 5,000-horsepower, five-cylinder Skinner installed in the laker *William P. Snyder, Jr.* in 1950. It is still there, powering the same vessel, which became the cement carrier *Medusa Challenger* in 1967.

Today the *Challenger* and the Canadian self-unloader *James Norris* are the only cargo vessels powered by unaflows in service on the lakes. The former railroad car ferry, *Badger*, which was returned to service on Lake Michigan after an eighteen month hiatus on May 15, 1992, is the world's only active passenger carrying vessel powered by unaflow engines. The last passenger-carrying American steamboat to have been built with these engines appears to have been the steamer/ferry *Naushon*, which was launched as the *Nantucket* in 1957.

During the period following World War II, many an old laker was repowered. Beginning with the *Charles S. Hebard* in 1948, Skinner unaflows replaced conventional triples in some twenty vessels. By this time, however, the diesel had become the almost universal engine of choice. The unaflow, despite its sophisticated technology, was already an anachronism. The last boat on the lakes, if not the world, to be converted to a unaflow was the Maritime-class *Frank Armstrong*, which was repowered in 1960 with an engine built in 1944. It is ironic that the last reciprocating steam engine to be placed in an American commercial vessel should replace one of the very last triple-expansion engines ever built. The following year saw the last conversion to steam on the lakes, when the *Charles M. Schwab* was repowered with a turbine. Since then, all conversions have been to diesel power.

Most of the old lakers, including many that were repowered, have not fared well since the fortunes of the region began to decline. Things are not the same on the Great Lakes today as they were a generation ago, and endeavors like steelmaking and mining are no longer the bulwark of our industrial strength. Recently, literally hundreds of old lake steamers have been scrapped—not because they were unsound, but because they were unused. Today only a handful remain. For those, it is not just the eleventh hour. It is 11:59.

CHAPTER 2

The veteran lake steamer *S. T. Crapo* is a working boat plain and simple. Her long life has been spent in the most mundane of occupations, hauling cement from her homeport in Alpena, Michigan, to various plants around the Great Lakes. The *Crapo* never ranked with the illustrious vessels of the world. Her gross tonnage is only 4,769 and her length overall is 402.60 feet—small by the standards of the Great Lakes today, where boats are considered "little" if they are under 730 feet long. She was built for the Huron Cement Company and launched on December 15, 1927, at the ship-yards of the Great Lakes Engineering Works at River Rouge, Michigan. Unlike most vessels of her age, she is unique in that she has been employed in the same service and has remained virtually unaltered since the day she was christened.

While she steamed away through the years anonymously, time worked in the *Crapo's* favor. Despite her advancing age, she was perfectly suited to the cement trade, where speed was of no consequence, and where she did not have to compete with newer, larger vessels that have come to dominate the lakes in recent years.

The *Crapo's* fame rests with the fact that she is a survivor, a remnant of the technology of the Industrial Revolution. She is coal fired, as were virtually all steamboats at the time of her construction—which in this day and age makes her an anachronism of the first degree. Today, aside from the *Badger* and two summer excursion steamers, the *Sabino* and the *Segwun*, she is alone on this continent. In fact, as far as is known, there are no coal burners on the high seas, nowhere except perhaps China, where steam propulsion is still a viable part of the transportation system. She is still generating steam in her original plant, old firetube Scotch boilers, no less. Her staunch old triple-expansion engine—for years the standard means of marine propulsion—is, as of 1992, one of two powering merchant vessels on this continent. And hers is the last true steam whistle to be heard on all of the lakes.

Like the last veterans of a war—who are more often the foot soldier and the drummer boy, not the great and illustrious—the *Crapo's* distinction lies in the fact that she has outlived most of her kind. By default, if nothing else, she has attained the rank of a classic among the vessels of the world.

Given my long association with the *Crapo*, it seemed inevitable that one day I would make a trip aboard her. So at 3:25 A.M. "boat time," on July 8, 1990, I found myself in her pilothouse, waiting to depart from the LaFarge Corporation's cement plant in Milwaukee, Wisconsin, bound for Alpena. Captain Howard Fisher, a veteran of forty years' service on the Great Lakes, was in command, steam was up and we were set to sail.

LaFarge's plant is located amid the grain elevators and railroad yards on the flats at the far end of the Burnham Canal, just west of downtown Milwaukee. In truth, the canal is nothing more than a twisting, narrow, shallow creek, where one might go fishing for bullheads. It is quite inconceivable that a vessel 400 feet long and sixty feet wide could find its way there from Lake Michigan. Be that as it may, the *Crapo* does find her way there, unloads her cargo, and then *backs* all the way out to the turning basin at the mouth of the harbor before heading out onto the lake. All this is old hat to the *Crapo* and her crew. They have been doing it year in and year out on an average of once a week from ice-out in the early spring to the end of December.

As if the problem of keeping from running aground were not enough, there are seven bridges in the *Crapo's* path, which must all be opened. At this hour, there are no bridge tenders on duty at two of the railroad bridges, so one must be summoned especially to open them.

"What time did you order the bridge for us?" Captain Fisher asked First Mate Gerald Beatty.

"Three o'clock."

"Better try to raise them again. We don't want them to get mad at us, 'cause we're late."

At 3:30, the wheelsman arrives. Captain Fisher turns off the lights in the pilothouse and picks up a walkie-talkie.

"O.K., we're all set up forward. Send that fellow aft," he says, referring to the tug *Bonnie Selvic*, which will be towing us from astern. Then he notices that the stack is not lit, and he orders the floodlights to be turned on, "so they'll know who we are."

At 3:38, a voice breaks in over the walkie-talkie announcing that the stern lines are in. From below I hear the thumping and wheezing of an old steam winch as it begins to pull in the bow lines.

"O.K., Wendell, she's all yours," Captain Fisher tells the captain of the tug.

"Better blow for that bridge again so they don't get an idea to close it on us," he adds.

I hear the whistle of the tug trying to rouse the bridge tender, and I look aft as a thin line of coal smoke begins to pour forth from the *Crapo's* stack. Out of the corner of my eye, I see a shadow move almost imperceptibly. It is 3:39. I look again and see the wall of the cement plant begin to slip past. I realize we are underway. Our departure is so effortless that there is no sensation of being in motion. It is as if we were standing still, as if the earth were being drawn away from beneath us ever so slowly. There is no sense of struggle such as with a plane striving to gain altitude on takeoff.

And so, with the tug *Bonnie Selvic* at the stern, and Captain Fisher in command, the *Crapo* begins to thread the needle through Milwaukee's waterways on her way to Lake Michigan.

No sooner are we underway than the voices of the deckhands over walkie-talkies begin to inform the captain of the *Crapo*'s progress.

"About 36 feet off the rudder," says one, letting him know the distance between the stern and the creek's bank.

"About 3 on the starboard, cap'n," another tells him, meaning that there are only 3 feet between the hull amidships and the shore.

"About 5 feet now aft."

"Got any clearance on that bridge?" the captain asks.

"Yeah, about 5 feet starboard aft," another voice answers.

I look back just in time to see the tug disappear behind a clump of trees as the *Crapo* begins to negotiate the right-angle bend before the first bridge.

"How far are you off, Dave?"

"About 2 feet, cap'n."

"Oh, Lord."

I watch incredulously as the bridge looms into view and we start to pass through the channel between its piers. A voice announces that we have no more than 2 feet of clearance amidships.

"Not going to be able to help you much here, Wendell. So you'll have to be ready," Captain Fisher informs the tug captain succinctly.

"Are we going to clear, Jimmy?"

"About 3 feet at starboard bow, cap."

"O.K., real good."

Nobody says a word until we have passed through unscathed.

"Better blow for the next bridge, Wendell."

Once again, the sound of the tug's whistle echoes over the predawn stillness of the sleeping city. A few minutes later, we pass between the uplifted leaves of the second bridge. The only sign that someone else is awake are the trucks high above us on the highway viaduct, and the lights of a lone car shimmering on the wet pavement of the street leading to the bridge. Our progress is so slow that, until I notice that objects on the shore are not in the same place as they were the last time I looked, it is hard to tell if we are moving at all. It is rather like watching the minute hand of a clock, which advances without the eye ever seeing it move.

As we approach the bend opposite the post office, where we enter the Menominee River, Jimmy's voice informs the captain: "We got no clearance off the starboard bow."

"I'm going to push her off," answers Captain Fisher, as he starts the bow thruster.

"Still no clearance starboard bow, cap'n."

"Wendell, you're going to have to pull us over. I got nothing to do with it now."

"How are you, Jimmy?"

"About 10 feet starboard aft. Looking good, captain."

"She's looking good."

"She's looking good, cap'n."

I step out and stand by the railing as we round the bend with what seems not an inch to spare amidships. I wouldn't have believed such a maneuver was possible unless I'd been there to see it myself. We have turned a full 90 degrees in less distance than the *Crapo*'s length.

"Davey, how we doing on port bow?" queries the captain.

"Twelve feet."

"O.K., Davey."

"I'm going to have to slow down. You'll have to pull, Wendell."

"O.K."

"I'm going to put her on warm-up, Wendell. She's picking up a lot of speed."

"Sounds good."

Captain Fisher rings "slow ahead" on the engine-room telegraph, the Chadburn; he waits a long minute to sense if the *Crapo* responds.

"I'm just riding, Wendell. Got the engine on warm-up now. That ought to slow her down."

I poured myself another cup of coffee and sat back on a stool to marvel at this tour de force of shipbuilding. Up to this point, it should be mentioned, the engine has just been turning over, on what's occasionally called "dead slow astern." All this intricate maneuvering has been done by the tug and the bow thruster under the aegis of Captain Fisher.

The bow thruster is "one of the best damned things that ever happened," to use the words of the captain of another lake freighter. It takes the place of a tug at the head of a vessel and is one of the most valuable tools at the captain's disposal. Since its adoption some twenty years ago, it has revolutionized shiphandling, as it virtually doubles a vessel's maneuverability. The thruster, itself, is a reverse-pitch propeller mounted athwartships in a tubular tunnel abaft the ship's stem, just above the bottom of the hull. It is controlled from the pilothouse and can be used either independently or in conjunction with the engine.

The first vessels on the Great Lakes to be so equipped were

the *J. R. Sensibar* and the *J. F. Schoellkopf, Jr.*, both of which were retrofitted with thrusters in 1961. The thruster quickly proved to be such a boon that since then, it has become standard equipment on virtually every lake freighter.

At one point, we pass so close to the buildings bordering the river that I feel as if I could reach out and touch them. As we approach the third bridge, a chorus of bells rises from the guard gates being lowered across the roadway. Here, as at the second bridge, there is a lone car waiting on the street for us to pass. Its driver is standing beside it, arms akimbo on the open door. As the *Crapo* comes abreast, he waves nonchalantly and calls out something to Dave.

After we pass safely through the bridge, Captain Fisher asks Dave if he left any paint on it.

"Yeah, but not too much."

"You made my day."

After a few minutes, Captain Fisher tries to contact the tender at the next bridge by radio: "S. T. *Crapo* to Soo Line Menominee Railroad Bridge on 10."

No answer.

"S. T. *Crapo* to Soo Line Menominee Railroad Bridge on 10."

Still no answer.

"Wendell, maybe you better blow. I can't raise 'em."

"O.K. I'll give them a toot."

And so it went until 4:39, an hour to the minute since we'd left the cement plant, when we passed through the seventh and last bridge. As we approached the turning basin, Captain Fisher called security on the radio to inform them that the steamer S. T. *Crapo* would be outbound in fifteen minutes.

"O.K., Wendell, toss her off anytime," he says, referring to the tow line.

"O.K., cap."

"Thanks a lot, and take care of yourself. Easy money tonight. Keep this up and you'll make more than your wife does selling real estate."

At 4:42, Jimmy announces that the towline is off. We are on our own. Captain Fisher goes to the Chadburn and rings "half astern"; then, after a minute, "stop"; then "slow ahead." He tells the wheelsman to "put on some right."

At 4:47 A.M., the *Crapo* straightens out and starts to head out to sea. As we pass under the Skyway Bridge, Captain Fisher rings "full ahead," and the throbbing of the old triple begins in earnest.

At 4:55 A.M., we steamed through the breakwall and onto Lake Michigan.

"Kind of a dark morning," remarks Bob Hensley, the wheelsman now on watch. "She's a little sloppy."

"Can you read Lake Michigan?" Captain Fisher asks Bruce Matthes, the mate, referring to the weatherfax.

"Yeah, cap'n. Three- to five-foot waves."

"What direction?"

"Doesn't say."

"Put her on 80, Bob. We'll wait until we're on the 32 course, to see what the A.M. weather has to tell us, before we start to pump."

The *Crapo* is *in ballast*, the term used for a ship that is not loaded with cargo. Whenever a vessel is being unloaded, water must be pumped into the ballast tanks around the sides and beneath its hull in order to maintain its stability. An empty vessel, or one with little ballast, rides high in the water and is more susceptible to the effects of wave action and the wind. Being lighter, however, enables it to make better speed. Captain Fisher, then, must wrestle with the question of speed versus a comfortable ride; whether to pump out some water from the tanks or keep them full.

Silence falls again while the captain sizes up the lake. It's still dark. The only audible sound is the creaking of the wheel as Bob works it back and forth, and the hum of the gyrocompass.

"Make her left to 32, Bob," Captain Fisher finally says. "Let's see how she rides."

After a few minutes, Captain Fisher finally makes the decision not to pump out the ballast tanks, explaining that being high in the water would make the ride too uncomfortable.

"Still a little sloppy out here. Besides, we've got a passenger," he says, looking in my direction with a smile.

We all laughed, and I asked how the *Crapo* rides.

"Like a dream," Bob answered without hesitation in his Carolinian drawl. "Just a nice roll. It'll rock you to sleep this morning."

"Well, I can't believe this thing rolls with a one-foot sea, but she does," answers Bruce.

After a few minutes, Captain Fisher gets up from his chair, stretches, and starts down the stairway leading to his cabin.

"See you tomorrow. I'm going to get some sleep."

The welcome smell of fresh, hot coffee begins to fill the pilothouse. Bob points to a well-used mug from the rack and tells me it is mine for the rest of the trip. I fill it to the brim and pull up a stool in front of a window on the opposite side from the captain's chair, which was to become my spot for the next three days.

Dawn begins to break at a little after five, revealing a gray, monochromatic world where sky and water are indistinguishable. We have passed gently from night to day, from one place to another, at a steady 12 miles per hour, leaving the rest of the world behind. Up here in the pilothouse, it is as if we were suspended in time and space. It is a sanctuary that seems impervious to change—a beautiful, silent space where, with the windows pulled down, you can feel the wind on your face. It is especially so this muted morning, for there are no blinding beams of sunlight to jar the senses. The only indication that we are moving at all is the steady, unmistakable throbbing of a steam engine.

The *Crapo's* pilothouse is comparatively small, and, like those on all old lakers, it is perched far forward on the "Texas deck." Up here, one has the feeling of being in an aerie, which is not surprising, for it is entirely surrounded by windows—in the *Crapo's* case, a total of seventeen. Despite its light and airy aura, the *Crapo's* is a far cry from the simple, uncluttered pilothouses that Mark Twain, or Captain Fisher as a young man, would have known. I am struck immediately by the many examples of old and new technologies that are represented here: Loran, the most sophisticated radar, and weather-forecasting instruments alongside the old brass and woodwork.

The centerpiece of all pilothouses is the wheel stand, on which the wheel itself is located. The *Crapo's* is a raised, oval platform surrounded by a heavy, polished-brass railing. Directly behind and a little to the left of the wheel is the wheelsman's perch, a high heavy oak chair that obviously has seen many years of use. At the front of the stand is the binnacle, a tall brass column housing the magnetic compass, on either side of which are the "gimbal balls"—red on the port side, green on starboard. These are used to offset the vessel's own magnetism, which otherwise would distort the compass readings. However, as a general rule, today the wheelsman steers by the gyrocompass, which is placed just forward and to the left of the wheel. The gyro is an electric compass, which unlike the magnetic compass, gives true North.

The most distinctive piece of equipment in the pilothouse of every steamboat is the engine-room telegraph—known throughout the Great Lakes as the "Chadburn," after the name of the British firm Chadburn and Company, which first manufactured it. It is one of the hallmarks of a true steamboat.

The captain of a steam vessel does not control the engine directly, as they do on large and recently built ships powered by diesel engines. It is the engineer below decks who actually operates the machine. Communication between the two is effected by means of the telegraph, a device which looks somewhat like a huge brass alarm clock with a moveable handle on top. The captain indicates what speed and direction he desires: full ahead, half ahead, full astern, half astern, etc., by moving the handle, which in turn moves a pointer on the dial of the Chadburn to the appropriate command. The identical message is repeated on the Chadburn in the engine room. The engineer adjusts the engine accordingly and then acknowledges the pilothouse by moving the pointer on his Chadburn to the same place indicated by the captain's command. Obviously, the cooperation between the two has to be precise to a degree. It is hard enough to control a vessel by oneself, but two people act as one on a steamboat. Before the invention of the telegraph, communication between pilothouse and engine room was achieved by a system of bells. The captain would ring a certain set of bells, indicating his desires, and the engineer would have to remember the sequence in which they were given and respond accordingly.

Sitting here on my stool sipping coffee, I begin to make a mental inventory of everything else in the pilothouse. It is crammed with just about every navigational device, as well as myriad other things that in some way or another are deemed essential. There are two Loran programmers and two radarscopes—one state-of-the-art instrument as well as a much earlier model, now used only as a spare. On the ceiling over the radar is a brand-new Ross Digital Depth Finder, model 5200B. Next to it, hanging from the handle of the searchlight control, is a plastic cup to keep water from dripping onto the radar. On top of the window in front of me is the original Weston model 273 rpm indicator, its needle wavering one side or the other of 85—"full ahead" for the *Crapo's* engine. Two big brass handles, not unlike an old-fashioned kitchen pump, are fastened to the floor under the middle window. These are used to operate the working whistle by which commands are given to the engineer if the Chadburn should fail. There are separate controls for the main whistle, the electric whistle, and the whistle timer. There are two pairs of binoculars—one for the captain and another for the mate—a weatherfax, a 16-inch oscillating fan, a brass clock, a calendar, three fire extinguishers, two VHF radios, a copy of *Greenwood's and Dill's Lake Boats '90*, a broom, a fly swatter, a cellular phone, and—on top of a two-drawer file cabinet—a Mr. Coffee coffeemaker.

At the back of the pilothouse is an enormous table on which are spread several charts of Lake Michigan. Stored beneath it are drawers with charts of every harbor and literally every inch of the Great Lakes system.

Directly over the starboard door is a framed copy of *Pilot Rules for the Great Lakes and Their Connecting and Tributary Waters.* and next to it, a framed NOTICE—Station Bills, Drills and Reports of Masters. Treasury Dept., U.S. Coast Guard CG-809, dated 11/53.

At the head of the stairway leading directly below to the captain's quarters are the framed licenses for the captain and each of the three mates. Next to these is the *Crapo's* Certificate of Inspection, also framed, dated 14 March 90, with an expiration date of 14 March 92. It informs me that the *Crapo's* last hull inspection was March 1988, which means that she is certified to operate until March 1993. In addition to providing information about where and when, her tonnage and length, it cites that her official number is D226885 and her call sign is WB6252. It also says that she is designated as a "freight ship," that her hull material is steel, that her engine is rated at 1,800 horsepower, the propulsion is steam reciprocating. The total number of persons allowed aboard is forty.

"Doesn't take much to make this old girl do a swan dance," remarks Bruce.

The seas are a bit rougher now. Bob was right, she could rock you to sleep. The atmosphere in the pilothouse was becoming almost soporific until, without warning, we were caught in a trough, slapped broadside by a hefty wave. The jolt barely made the *Crapo* shudder, but it was a reminder of Lake Michigan's volatile nature, which can be riled up on a moment's notice. Six-foot seas are nothing to the *Crapo*. Those of 10 feet are manageable, but when they get to be 15 feet, it's best to find a place to hide and "drop the hook."

"I'll bet that will bring the old man up," says Bruce.

It did. In less than a minute, Captain Fisher was in the pilothouse sizing up the situation.

"Pull her up a little, Bob, so when we get to Point Sable we can change to 30. That way, we can eat dinner without getting soup in our laps."

In no time at all, the *Crapo* gains her footing and is rolling along at a steady, even gait through sloppy, 6-foot seas on a new course of 38 degrees, heading diagonally toward the Michigan coast.

Once he senses that the *Crapo* is taking everything in stride, Captain Fisher settles down in his immense, oversize Naugahyde chair. He sits there looking silently out at the lake for a long time, keeping his thoughts to himself. I knew that he was considering taking his pension after another season or two. I wondered what it must be like to have spent the better part of a lifetime out here on the lakes, and then to contemplate the idea of retiring—to sit in another chair, so to speak. Would it be a relief after so many years of carrying the burden of responsibility for crew and vessel, or would the passage of the days, themselves, become a burden once the novelty of being carefree wore off? Would the sedentary life—or even that of a peripatetic voyeur—suffice after so many years of being in command?

I once asked another captain on the eve of his retirement what he would like to do most of all. "Be able to get a full night's sleep," he replied without hesitation.

After what seemed a long time, Captain Fisher suddenly stood up and spoke good-naturedly to nobody in particular on his way below to his cabin: "It's hot up here. Got the heat turned up or is it just Bob sweating?"

After he had gone, I remembered what I had been told about the starboard side of a vessel being solely the captain's domain. According to tradition, it was his and his alone to walk upon. But as "Bud" Tambourski, the captain of the steamer *J. Burton Ayers*, had said to me, "It seems all the traditions are changing each time a new man comes on board."

It's true; most traditions associated with steamboating, like everything else, seem to have gone the way of the boats themselves. However, here on the *Crapo*, at least one is still honored: The chair on the right side of the pilothouse is exclusively for the captain's use. And Captain Tambourski on his commands still has the wheelsman ring the bells every fifteen minutes in his pilothouse, "just to keep everyone on their toes."

At 11:08, the car ferry *Badger* appeared out of the haze 4.5 miles away, bearing 44 degrees, laying down a heavy trail of coal smoke.

In how many places in the world today can one see two coal-fired steamboats passing each other, I asked myself? In July 1990, the *Badger*, the *Irvin L. Clymer*, and the *Crapo* were the only ones abroad on the Great Lakes.

As I watched the *Badger* steaming past our stern on her way to Kewaunee, Wisconsin, I remembered the time when it was commonplace to see a line of coal smoke being drawn across the horizon. The old *Badger*, with a little stretch of the imagination, could as well have been any steamer, and I could, just as well, have been on the Mediterranean as on Lake Michigan. I followed the *Badger's* progress until she was barely visible in the haze, merely a chimera. In my mind's eye, I saw legions of old engines pounding away below decks as they had for generations without respite on God knows how many ships. I imagined, too, sweaty men feeding coal to the fires in the searing heat of the stokeholds of a thousand steamers.

Extraordinary, too, it seemed, that all the smoke, which now hung like a thin black contrail across the sky as far as one could see, should come from a single stack. How insignificant the *Badger* was in comparison to what it had left behind; improbable, too, that something so small could leave such a mark. Much like man himself, I thought. Viewed in the larger context, the smoke that now hung there in the sky long after the old car ferry passed over the horizon did not simply mark the course of the *Badger's* passage. It could, as well, have marked the course of civilization.

In a day and age when the world runs on oil, it is hard to imagine that once coal was king. For more than a century, it fueled the commerce of the world, fed the furnaces that drove our ships and the locomotives that hauled everything we made and used. Although coal and steam together were the driving forces upon which the industrial age was founded, as a team they did not survive the rigors of technological evolution in the world of transportation—all but here, at least, where on this Sunday morning in July 1990, there was the illusion that both were hard at work for us.

Coal and the Great Lakes have had a long association with one another. Coal has been used here as a fuel for vessels longer than anywhere else on this side of the world. In fact, up until 1949 all "lakers" were built as coal burners, and coal-burning boats were still being built for lake service up until the mid-1950s. The *Badger* and her sistership, the *Spartan*, launched in 1953 and 1952, respectively, were among the very last American coal-fired ships ever built. Coal was cheap and plentiful on the lakeshore, and, as the second-largest cargo carried by the lake freighters, it stood to reason that it should also be used to fuel them. There were other factors, too. Many a shipping and coal company were intertwined in some corporate fashion that provided an added incentive to burn it. But one of the main reasons coal burners remained as long as they did on the lake was the same one that kept most lakers alive for so many years—fresh water. The boats themselves lasted.

Today coal smoke is in ill repute. Not only are coal burners environmentally unacceptable, they also are uneconomical, requiring more manpower: firemen, plus additional wipers. In the days before stokers, which feed coal into the furnaces automatically, all coal burners were hand fired, and thus even more uneconomical, as they required extra firemen and the services of coal passers as well. In time, too, all coal-fired boilers reached the point where their age alone made them increasingly inefficient. Today, virtually all steam vessels that once burned coal have been reboilered with automated oil-fired furnaces, which require no firemen at all. In most cases, steam was dispensed with altogether, and the vessel was converted to diesel.

The demise of coal-burning boats has resulted in the abandonment of virtually all the coaling stations along the lakeshores. Today, the only place where the *Crapo* can regularly take on coal is at Alpena, her homeport. Her bunkers carry 300 tons "level full," 350 if "heaped." She burns between 36 and 40 tons a day, which means she carries enough coal for nine and a half days of normal steaming. Since she calls at Alpena to load cement on an average of every five days or less, this usually is more than enough fuel, at least in the summer. I remember one November, however, when stormy weather had forced her to spend five days at anchor en route to Milwaukee. Once there, another storm blew up, and she spent two more days in port waiting for the winds to abate. When she finally left, she had less than 80 tons of fuel on board—enough to get her safely home unless the weather turned against her again.

When I was a boy, the smell of coal smoke was the elixir of adventure. I had never heard the word *pollution*. Things are simpler when you are eleven or twelve. Although I didn't understand the significance of such things, the connotation of coal smoke was different then. It was the gauge of prosperity, an indication that all our forces had been mustered and were working full ahead with singular purpose. Furnaces roaring white hot, smoke belching from every stack—these were looked upon with great pride as signs of full employment, as signs that good times were at hand.

I looked up at the line of smoke swirling from the *Crapo's* stack and saw the *Badger's* contrail still plainly visible hanging in the sky far astern. They were no longer just symbolic of a magnificent functionalism. Once back on dry land, I would have to see them in another, darker light.

Captain Fisher was good to his word: No soup was spilled in our laps during lunch. Afterward, I stood by the rail on the Texas deck below the pilothouse, looking out across the unbroken expanse of water and sky—as one is wont to do on a voyage—and marveled at the wonder of being on an inland sea. The sensation was almost more phenomenal than on the ocean, where it is a matter of course to be out of sight of land for days or even weeks. Here, too, the earth was water. At the moment, there was no hint of the land that lay all around us, the land that defined these waters as lakes.

At one point during the passage, a lone gull appeared and followed our wake. How odd, I thought at first, to see a gull so far out; it should have been a storm petrel, or some other pelagic bird. But no, of course not, we were in the middle of Lake Michigan. To one born and raised on the Atlantic Ocean, gulls belong on the seacoast. This one seemed almost as great an anomaly as those that follow farmers plowing the fields of North Dakota, picking up insects from the freshly turned soil.

I looked down at the deep blue-green water riven by the passage of the hull and felt a pang of sadness for myriad steamers I have known, and the era that is gone. Almost gone. The reassuring throbbing of the *Crapo's* old triple-expansion engine still kept it alive.

In my mind's eye, I saw New York Harbor as it used to be—an exciting, stirring place, charged with energy, so unlike the way it is today. Steam whistles, shrill and deep, reverberated from its every corner, as they still do from the memories of my youth. I remember that when I was in school, there were so many ferry lines in the harbor that it was impossible to ride them all in a day. There were tugs of every description and lighters steaming this way and that, scuttling to dodge the great liners on their way to the North River piers. I remember the "palatial steel steamers" of the Hudson River Day Line, which sped effortlessly up and down the river each summer. I knew them all and greeted them like old friends every season: the paddlewheelers *Alexander Hamilton*, *Robert Fulton*, and *Hendrick Hudson*, and the others, too—the *De Witt Clinton*, *Peter Stuyvesant*, and the little *Chauncey M. Depew*. I was familiar with the trim, tall-stacked coastal steamers, like the *Nobska*, which frequented the waters of New England, and the beautiful *City of Keansburg*, which steamed away to the Jersey coast on hot summer weekends.

For a time when I was a very little boy, my bedroom window looked out on New York's East River. I would sit there for hours, mesmerized by an endless stream of vessels of every description. The river teemed with activity, as in the paintings of Reginald Marsh or the photographs of Berenice Abbott. I ate my supper by the window every night, looking out at the city and the bridges, watching the lights come up and the boats slipping by quietly on the river.

Every evening there came a parade of night boats—the *Comet*, the *Arrow*, and the *Evangeline*—bound for New England down Long Island Sound. I remember as if it were yesterday the time my father waved his newspaper from the deck of one of the "Boston boats" as it passed beneath the window. Then, as the twilight deepened, up the river came the Rye Beach boat, all lit up with its decks lined with humanity leaning over the rails, and the sound of the band playing. And during the 1939 World's Fair, every excursion boat in New York must have passed by my window.

On winter afternoons, the light was cold and clear, like Charles Sheeler's paintings. Everywhere were little puffs of steam coming from the buildings, and the smokestacks of the boats, as if the city were breathing—evidence that it was an organism. From what I saw through the window, I learned of the effect of light and shadow on objects; about architecture and magnificent bridges; and most of all about boats.

It wasn't until much later that I came to know the Great Lakes and to discover that they had a formidable maritime history of their own, having been home to some of the world's most unique vessels. Even today, despite my long association with them, I still find it almost incomprehensible to fathom the idea of a fleet of huge ships plying landlocked seas in the middle of a continent a thousand miles or more from the open ocean.

Be that as it may, over the course of time all manner of vessels evolved to serve the specific needs of the lake-borne traffic: ore carriers, grain boats, whalebacks, car ferries, self-unloaders. Nor did the lakes have a dearth of other, more conventional vessels. There were tugs, and lighters, too—even lightships. In summer, flotillas of excursion steamers called at almost every port. Every night, huge three-funnelled paddlewheelers churned up Lake Erie's waters. Vest-pocket liners (some even built on Scotland's Clydebank), which rivaled their oceanic counterparts in all respects of luxury and service, steamed in and out of port throughout the lakes. The last boat train—a train dedicated to carrying passengers to and from ports of embarkation—in the world ran not between London and Southampton to meet the *Queen Mary*, as one might expect, but from Toronto to quayside at Port McNicoll on Georgian Bay, there to meet the Canadian Pacific's magnificent *Assiniboia* and *Keewatin*.

But the most distinctive of all were the bulk cargo carriers, like the *S. T. Crapo*, which for more than a century have been the workhorses of the lakes.

The adage "Form follows function" was never more appropriate than when applied to marine architecture. The shape of every steamboat—all vessels, for that matter—is determined essentially by what it does and where it is used—never more so than with the design of the Great Lakes bulk freighter—a type of vessel and a form of marine architecture found nowhere else in the world.

The concept of the laker was first promulgated by Captain Eli Peck of Cleveland, who in 1869 designed and built the progenitor of all such vessels, the 217-foot wooden-hulled *R. J. Hackett*. Peck's design was a radical departure from anything previously seen on the Great Lakes—or, for that matter, anywhere else—a vessel that would provide maximum cargo space and would be able to load and unload as quickly as possible. The result was a boat that has been described as "an island with a house at each end." All these "straight-deckers," as they came to be called, were characterized by a long, unbroken, sweeping hull, and a deck where hatches were placed from one end of it to the other. It was punctuated by a pilothouse at one end and an "after" house at the other, beneath which was the engine room and firehold. It had a single screw in the center protected by the rudder, rather than two on each side—where, Peck surmised, they could be damaged in shallow waters. Because propellers were not as fast as paddlewheels, Peck correctly reasoned that his boat would need a larger engine

An even more radical departure from conventional marine design was the placement of the engine far aft to allow for as much cargo space as possible. Here Peck was more prescient than he realized: Today all cargo vessels, not just those on the Great Lakes, are designed as "after-enders." The pilothouse was placed well forward over the point of the bow, far ahead of the area that could be used for cargo. Unlike other lake vessels of the time, and all oceangoing craft—which until very recently have been characterized by sleek lines and knifelike prows—the hull of the laker is square, of shallow draft, and broad of beam.

Needless to say, Peck's design was a success. In time, the Great Lakes bulk-cargo fleet became the largest merchant navy in the world dedicated to a single trade.

Quite apart from its function as the ultimate bulk-cargo freighter, the laker was a completely different vessel from its counterparts on the high seas. It had to be designed with the lakes' notorious storms in mind. Ocean waves are large and comparatively sluggish, but the combination of less dense fresh water and shorter fetch on the lakes produces quick, choppy seas with shorter wavelengths. As a result, it often is possible to have two or three waves under a ship at the same time. In storms where mountainous waves of 15 to 20 feet are commonplace, and those of 30 or 40 feet are not unheard of, unprecedented stresses can be produced that can overwhelm all but the stoutest vessel.

The next landmark in the design of the "laker" came in 1882, thirteen years after the *Hackett*, with the launching of the first iron-hulled carrier, *Onoko*, considered by most to be the prototype of the modern bulk carrier on the lakes. This was followed in 1886 by the construction of the *Spokane*, the lake's first steel-hulled bulk freighter. The next milestone in the evolution of the laker came when U.S. Steel's Pittsburgh Steamship Company launched the ore carrier *J. Pierpont Morgan* in 1906. This was the first of the so-called "600 footers," the prototype for a class of vessel that became the mainstay of the Great Lakes fleet for the next thirty-five years. By the standard of the day, these were leviathans, indeed, "being the largest coarse freighters in the world."

An even greater quantum leap came two years later, with the advent of the self-unloader, which until recently was a type of vessel unique to the Great Lakes. The self-unloader was conceived by George B. Palmer, chief engineer of the Wyandotte Chemicals Corporation. Although the *Hennepin*, which was converted to a self-unloader in 1902, technically is the first of its kind, the first vessel so designed was, logically, the *Wyandotte*, built for Palmer's firm in 1908. Palmer's con-

cept revolutionized the whole process of discharging a vessel's cargo, and it eventually changed the nature of lake shipping itself. The great advantage of a self-unloader is that the process can be accomplished virtually anyplace where the boom can reach the shore. Theretofore, expensive and elaborate onshore machinery had been necessary for removing cargo from the holds of a conventional straight-decker.

While there are several variations, the principle of a self-unloader is simplicity itself. It consists of a system of one or two conveyors, which carry the cargo from beneath the vessel's holds to a boom mounted on the deck. The boom, which is equipped with an endless belt, is swung ashore, where the cargo is discharged onto the ground. Initially, self-unloaders were smaller boats generally used for hauling stone and coal. It wasn't until the advent of pelletized ore, which could be removed from the cargo hold by self-unloading mechanisms, that self-unloaders replaced the conventional straight-decker in the iron-ore trade. Today, virtually all the remaining U.S.-flag bulk freighters have been converted to self-unloaders of one type or another, and since 1960, all new American vessels built on the lakes have been of this type. On the other hand, the majority of Canadian vessels, which are engaged in the grain trade, where self-unloading vessels are of no use, are straight-deckers.

For the next forty years after George Palmer's innovation, lakeboat size and design remained basically the same. The next landmark came in 1949, with the construction of Inland Steel's 678-foot *Wilfred Sykes*. Not only was she the first ore carrier on the lakes to be built with oil-fired boilers, but also her 7,000-horsepower turbine and 20,000-ton capacity made her by far the largest and most powerful of the lakers at the time. The decade of the fifties saw the advent of the first vessels over 700 feet in length and the last vessels with the conventional two-house configuration which still had the vestigial lines of the classic lake steamers.

The opening of the new Poe Lock on the Saint Marys Ship Canal between Lake Huron and Lake Superior at Sault Ste. Marie on June 26, 1969, at a stroke brought about the most profound effect on lakeboat design since the launching of Peck's *Hackett* a century earlier. The new lock, which was 1,200 feet long and 101 feet wide, could accommodate vessels far larger than anything seen previously on the lakes. The shipping companies wasted no time in taking advantage of the lock's dimensions. Two days later, ground was broken for the yard at Erie, Pennsylvania, that was to assemble the lakes' first 1,000-foot vessel, the *Stewart J. Cort*. With the launching of the *Cort*, the death knell had been sounded for all the old lakers.

Before the arrival of this new breed of diesel-powered

leviathan, many an old laker built in the first half of the century continued to steam away through the years, seemingly immune to progress. For years their contemporaries on the high seas had succumbed to the onslaught of technological change—slowly at first, one by one, then by battalions. Many others were sunk during two world wars and several lesser conflicts. Although steam survived on the Great Lakes longer than anywhere else in America, here, too, in time it began to fade. In recent years, ships have been sent to the breakers in droves. They were not scrapped because they were worn out. On the contrary, being on fresh water, their hulls could have survived almost indefinitely, as many had. They were scrapped because they were no longer economical and could not compete with the newer, larger ships, which could carry far more cargo, for lower rates, with the same-size crews. The situation was much the same as a "mom and pop" store trying to compete with a supermarket.

Once a fleet of steamers numbering in the hundreds set forth each spring. In 1992 one hundred and thirty-four of its total of 146 vessels are scheduled to sail on the Great Lakes. Thirty-eight are steamboats—twenty American and eighteen Canadian. Only four of these are powered by reciprocating engines—two by triples, the *Crapo* and the *Willowglen*, and two by unaflows, *The Medusa Challenger* and *The James Norris*. Diminished as their ranks may be, these boats still make up by far the largest fleet of commercial steam vessels in the Western Hemisphere. All but these few are turbine driven, and, being essentially of modern design, they bear little resemblance to those in this book. However, it is important to note that their numbers include some of the last steam-powered merchant vessels built in America. Interlake Steamship Company's *Herbert C. Jackson* and *Charles M. Beeghly*, both launched in 1959; Bethlehem Steel's *Arthur B. Homer*, since scrapped; and Inland Steel's *Edward L. Ryerson* in 1960 were the last American steamships built for the Great Lakes trade. The *Canadian Leader* of 1967, owned by the Canadian firm ULS International, was the very last lake steamer to be placed in service.

At 5:07 P.M., "Sleepy," Sleeping Bear Dune, emerges from the haze. We have been steaming out of sight of land in the midst of America for some eleven hours, 150 miles at 12.5 miles an hour, "full ahead" for the *S. T. Crapo*.

And it has been an empty lake, indeed, over which we have steamed. Save for the *Badger*, not a single vessel has been sighted.

"A quiet day for a Sunday," remarks Bruce. "Usually there are so many boaters out here talking to one another on the radio it drives you nuts."

Like all steamboatmen I have met, he regards pleasure craft as so much flotsam and a hazard to navigation, which in fact they have become in recent years.

"We don't have much of a merchant marine either anymore. Cuba's probably got a bigger one.

"Was a time you could look in the radar and see ten or twelve boats, big lakeboats. Now there's nothing. *Nothing.* It's a dying trade."

Perhaps. By comparison, in 1944 there were some 356 vessels in the American fleet alone, which had a combined carrying capacity of 3,238,000 gross tons. The statistics are somewhat misleading, however. In 1992, despite the fact there were only sixty-one bulk cargo carriers in the American fleet (fifty-nine were in service), they had a cargo capacity of 2,021,575 gross tons. The reason so few could carry so much is that the overall vessel size has increased dramatically. Since 1972, when the first of the 1,000-footers was placed in service, the number of U.S.–flag boats on the lakes, especially the smaller craft, has declined dramatically. The 600-footers, which once were the standard bulk carriers on the lakes, have an average cargo capacity of approximately 17,000 tons. Each of the thirteen 1,000-footers has an average capacity of 64,538 tons. Collectively, they can carry some 838,994 tons, the approximate equivalent of fifty vessels in the 600-foot category. This amounts to 42 percent of the total capacity of the entire U.S. Great Lakes fleet.

By comparison, the *Crapo's* capacity is 8,500 tons, far too small to be economically competitive with the 1,000-footers, which could carry seven times the *Crapo's* cargo if they were in the same business. The *Crapo*, and the other vessels owned by Inland Lakes management survive because they are in a highly specialized trade. They haul cement, and do it far more economically, over a much larger area, than the railroads and the trucking companies with whom they compete.

Looking out on the empty lake this evening, it is hard to believe that these sweetwater seas have been the keystone of America's industrial heartland for more than a century. Nonetheless, it is true. Over the years, hundreds of millions of tons of iron ore, coal, limestone, and grain were borne upon the lakes on bulk-cargo freighters. Burly, grimy old cities such as Cleveland, Detroit, and Chicago became the quintessential industrial centers. Duluth and Buffalo rivaled New York and Liverpool as ports. The Detroit River was said to be the busiest waterway in the world. Despite the fact that they were in operation only eight months out of the year, the Soo Locks, on the St. Marys River, between Lakes Superior and Huron, at one time handled four times the tonnage of the Suez Canal and six times that of the Panama Canal.

A pale sun briefly breaks out of the clouds, revealing a fogbank creeping across the lake ahead of us. By 5:28 P.M., we are in the midst of fog so dense that the *Crapo's* afterhouse has disappeared from view. Nothing but pea soup ahead, nothing beyond the end of the steering pole. Zero visibility now as the captain stands glued to the radar, and the *Crapo's* whistle speaks out every three minutes.

"What did you do before radar?" I ask Jerry, the mate.

"Run aground a lot. I dunno. I never sailed before radar. I'm a short-timer compared to some of the people around here. Twenty-one years, twenty-two coming up. The captain's been here over forty. Leonard, the chief, over fifty. I'll never make forty; twenty-five, maybe."

7:26. The fog begins to lift slightly.

"I can see a hundred miles," says Captain Fisher, looking up from the radar screen.

The afterhouse and the *Crapo's* tall stack reappear in the mist, like a ghost ship taking shape astern of us. The sun, behind the fogbank, suffuses everything with a soft yellow glow. As the fog begins to dissipate, a towering bank of thunderheads is revealed to the northwest—"a classic line squall, right there," remarks Captain Fisher, pointing in the direction of the storm, "and this is the worst place for one."

Bob reminds everyone of the time last year when lightning stuck the spar just aft of the pilothouse at the exact moment the mate stepped out of the door on the way to the head.

"Scared him so much he didn't go to the bathroom for three months."

"Thought it was a year," the captain said almost inaudibly, without lifting his eyes from the radar screen.

The sky darkens all around us, the thunder begins to crash, the rain is driven against the windows in sheets, the pilothouse shudders as the wind gusts—up to 45 knots, according to the anemometer. The lake begins to seethe before the force of the wind, as whitecaps build in intensity. Suddenly, everything beyond the windows is obliterated. I wait for the *Crapo* to begin to roll, as she did with a following sea earlier in the day, but now the wind is in her teeth she seems hardly to notice the squall at all.

As quickly as it came, it is gone, just a mite of a storm—a reminder, though, of what can happen out here on the lakes.

"Those grand freshwater seas of ours . . . possess an ocean-like expansiveness with many of the ocean's noblest traits . . . ," said Ishmael in *Moby Dick*. And some of the worst as well. "They are swept by Borean and dismasting blasts as direful as any that lash the salted wave. They know what shipwrecks are; for, out of sight of land, however inland, they have drowned many a midnight ship with all its shrieking crew."

Indeed. The winds were so direful on Lake Superior the night of November 10, 1975, that the pilot urged the master of the Swedish ship *Avafors* not to set out from Sault Ste. Marie, for he said it was "the wildest night I ever saw."

"Pilot," said the captain, "it's only the lakes."

Hours later, after having made little headway against 80-knot winds and 25-foot seas, he admitted, "We've got no business out here."

"I told you that, but it's too damn late," replied the pilot. "I would be scared to turn her around now."

The *Avafors* survived. The *Edmund Fitzgerald*, one of the proudest vessels ever to sail the lakes, did not. She was overcome by the horrendous seas just a few miles from where the *Avafors* was riding out the gale and went down with all hands so quickly that there was not even time to send an SOS.

Apart from the loss of the *Fitzgerald*, some of the worst shipwrecks in our history have occurred on the Great Lakes. Not too far from here, some 12 miles southwest of Gull Island, the *Carl D. Bradley* broke apart in mountainous seas and went down at a little before seven o'clock in the evening of November 18, 1958. Only two survived the fearful ordeal that night.

Dread, stormy November, the ship killer. The month when the infamous low-pressure systems sweep across the lakes almost like clockwork every three or four days, and when most vessels spend as much as a third of their time at anchor.

Beginning with the pioneer steamer *Walk-in-the-Water*, lost in a gale in 1821, November has claimed more lake vessels and lives of those who sailed them than any other month. Aside from the *Bradley* and the *Fitzgerald*, many have gone missing, simply "sailed through a crack in the lake," it has been said. The most devastating tempest of all was the "Great Storm" of November 13, 1913, which sent eleven boats and 250 men to their death at the bottom of Lake Huron and damaged or destroyed dozens of other vessels.

One would expect that the odds would be different on the ocean, that shipwrecks would be all part of the game. There the possibility of being lost seems very plausible, but hardly so on lakes surrounded by farms and forests, where the glow of city lights often is visible on the horizon at night. When one puts out to sea, there is always the chance that you will be overcome before reaching the next landfall. It is part of a tacit understanding between man and the elements on the open ocean. How peculiar, though, to contemplate the danger of foundering between Wisconsin and Michigan, when hardly ever out of sight of land on a sweetwater inland sea.

CHAPTER 3

As a port, Ashtabula may not be in a class with Yokohama or Bremerhaven, but it certainly has had its place in the sun. Many a tall-stacked steamer has called here. Over the years, hundreds of millions of tons of iron ore were unloaded from the holds of lake freighters at Ashtabula's docks and carried away by the trainload to the blast furnaces of Pittsburgh and the Ohio River Valley. But with the precipitous decline in steelmaking in recent years, Ashtabula's fortunes changed. Today its commerce is largely outbound. Iron ore, in the form of taconite pellets, may still be by far the largest cargo on the lakes—64,293,186 tons were carried in 1991—but coal has exceeded its importance as Ashtabula's main inbound cargo.

Like so many of Lake Erie's ports, Ashtabula's fortune now rests on "black diamonds." Coal in mile-long trains wends its way northward from mines deep in the hollows of Appalachia to be poured into the holds of the lakeboats—in 1991, some 5,337,594 tons, most of it bound for Canada, the rest for western lake ports such as Milwaukee. In point of fact, coal is second only to iron ore as a cargo on the lakes: 35,282,357 net tons of it were shipped in 1991.

Quite apart from its importance in the scheme of commerce on the lakes, Ashtabula seems a fit and proper port of embarkation for a journey over the inland seas on the grand old steamer *Crispin Oglebay*, for she was born here forty-seven years ago.

The *Oglebay* and her half-sister *The J. Burton Ayers* are among the six surviving examples of the Maritime-class vessels designed for service on the Great Lakes during World War II. Not only were these the very last steamboats built on the lakes with expansion engines, but also the last of the "600-footers," the freshwater leviathans of their day.

At the outset of the war, the American lake fleet was on the verge of obsolescence. Only nine new boats had been built since 1930. To ensure that the supply of vital war materials, especially iron ore, would not be interrupted, the U.S. Maritime Commission designed and built sixteen bulk-cargo carriers. All were launched in 1943 and were sold to eight separate shipping companies.

All of the Maritimes were virtually identical in length, beam, and depth—620 or 621 feet by 60 feet 3 inches by 35 feet—and had nearly the same tonnage. However, the similarity stops there. The ten L6-S-B1-class vessels, like the *Oglebay*, were built by the Great Lakes Engineering Works at Ashtabula, and at River Rouge, Michigan. All had the lines of the conventional laker, with counter sterns and tall stacks. All ten were powered by 2,500-horsepower, three-cylinder triple-expansion engines similar to those of the famous Liberty ships, which were built at the same time.

The six L6-S-A1-class vessels, like the *Ayers*, were constructed by the American Shipbuilding Company at Lorain and Cleveland, Ohio, and they differed in two very important aspects from the B1s. They were the first boats on the Great Lakes with cruiser sterns, a feature that was to set the trend for the design of subsequent lake freighters. More important, they were, as far as I know, the only steamers on the Great Lakes to be powered by a unique four-crank, double-compound Lenz Standard Marine Engine—essentially two separate engines placed end to end that power a common shaft. It seems somehow ironic that this German-designed engine was used to power American vessels during World War II.

The sole survivor of the L6-S-A1 class is the *Ayers*, which started life in Lorain as hull number 828 and made her maiden voyage from Lorain to Duluth on August 19, 1943. In 1974, she was sold to her present owner, the Columbia Transportation Division, Oglebay Norton Company.

The *Oglebay* began life as hull number 524—the next-to-last of the B1 class—at the shipyards of the Great Lakes Engineering Works in Ashtabula. She was launched as the Wilson Marine Transit's bulk freighter *J. H. Hillman, Jr.*, and she sailed away on her maiden voyage on September 27, 1943. For the next thirty years, she plied her trade as an ore and bulk-cargo carrier. She also joined the Columbia fleet in 1974 and was renamed *Crispin Oglebay*. At the same time, both she and the *Ayers* were converted to self-unloaders in Toledo, Ohio. In 1981, the *Oglebay* was laid up at Toledo, Ohio, where she remained inactive for the next eight years. Although most thought that she never would run again, she defied the prognosticators. She was reactivated, refitted, and returned to service in June 1989.

This will be the fifty-ninth trip for the *Oglebay* this season since her first on April 8. Thus far this year, she has steamed a total of 14,845 miles loaded and 10,043 miles "in ballast"—the equivalent of a round-the-world voyage, all on landlocked seas. By season's end, she will have made more than ninety-five trips and carried a prodigious 1,280,000 tons of cargo. Nonetheless, the *Oglebay* is small compared to today's lake leviathans.

The idea of a vessel more than 600 feet long, which can swallow the contents of a 120-car freight train in a single load, being considered small seems quite ludicrous. Most of the world's merchant ships, aside from supertankers and some of the larger cruise ships, are smaller, as were a fair share of the oceangoing passenger liners. I remember seeing the *Ayers* coming up the Calumet River in Chicago toward the KCBX coal dock late one night. As she loomed up in the dark, she looked almost as impressive as the *Queen Mary* steaming up the Narrows into New York Harbor.

As I watched the *Oglebay's* last hold being filled, I was reminded of what "Bud" Tambourski, captain of the *Ayers*, had told me during my trip on her earlier this summer.

"Loading is not a haphazard affair," he had said. "It's not just a matter of dumping cargo into the holds any old way. You notice how the operator on the loader moves in and out over the holds? That's so he can level the load and peak it. A seasoned mate knows exactly how much to put in each location and how to make piles of interlocking triangles for more stability.

"On every boat, you load fore and aft first, then the middle. If you put too much amidships, she'll 'belly'—bend down. If there's not enough, she'll 'hog'—bend upward. If she's hogged, you can work it out by adding a little more in the middle. You have to keep winching the boat back and forth along the dock to keep it even.

"The most seaworthy of ships is one with a full load of coal, because it fills up the whole hold and there is minimum shifting"—a reassuring thought to keep in mind as we steam toward Milwaukee loaded to our maximum summer draft with 13,244 tons of it.

In the distance, the remnants of a far-off thunderstorm, pink and purple, like giant Portuguese men-of-war, drift away over the lake toward Canada. The air is full of water vapor, as my father used to say when describing the quality of light after a storm. By contrast, the *Oglebay* herself is still moored securely to her industrial base. To the east, the view is dominated by a vast railroad yard filled with track after track of hopper cars. Beyond these lie mountains of limestone piled along the docks. In their midst, two huge new "after-enders" are unloading their cargo. From my vantage point, high above it all in the pilothouse, the view looks like an immense diorama filled with scale-model cars and ships. To the west, the scene is of a world of coal, piled in windrows on the ground, in lines of railroad cars, or stored in immense silos connected by a labyrinth of conveyors. Everything, even the mud, is sooty black. The buildings are stained from years of exposure to the infernal dust, which, despite sprinklers and the best efforts of all concerned, still pervades the atmosphere over every coal port from Norfolk to Newcastle.

At sunset, the *Oglebay* suddenly springs to life, awakened like some nocturnal creature about to set forth on the hunt. The winches begin to thump and hiss as the wires are brought in. Captain Bob Noffze and the Wheelsman "Bud" Larson arrive. All at once, the pilothouse, which has been as somnolent as a country church on Monday afternoon, becomes a command center. Orders are given in quick succession to the deck crew by walkie-talkie, the bow thruster is turned on—and a pot of freshly brewed coffee is ready and waiting.

How different the sailing of a lake freighter is from that of an ocean liner, which always is accompanied by much fanfare and many farewells. By contrast, the *Oglebay's* departure tonight is entirely unheralded. The only person on hand to bid us adieu is the wife of one of the crew members. As the *Oglebay* readies for its voyage, the rest of Ashtabula goes about its business. The comings and goings of boats are all part of a routine that has taken place in all of the Ashtabulas on the lake for as long as anyone can remember. There is nothing special about tonight's sailing, just another load of coal outbound. There is already another boat just beyond the breakwall anxious to take the *Oglebay's* place at quayside, and several more are downbound for Ashtabula out on Lake Erie. It is the *Oglebay* herself that makes tonight's sailing a special event, and only because this is September 1990. She and the *Ayers* are the last old lakers to make Ashtabula a regular port of call, whereas only twenty years ago, Ashtabula hosted myriad of their kind.

It is dark, except for the barely visible afterglow in the west, as the old self-unloader *Crispin Oglebay* moves serenely toward Lake Erie with a regal bearing befitting an ocean liner. There is not a sound. Ahead of us on the lake are the lights of the *H. B. White*, waiting for us to clear the channel. Flocks of gulls and terns aroused by our passage are caught by the beam of our searchlight as they take flight and disappear into the night. As we pass the lighthouse at the end of the breakwall, a cool breeze begins to blow through the open windows. I look at my watch. It's 9:32 P.M. Bob picks up the engine-room telephone and tells the engineer that he is "going to ring her up full," and to "work her up as you can."

I looked aft as we swung west in a wide arc, leaving Ashtabula astern. To the east, the moon, a fellow westering voyager, was setting forth as well—both of us to travel across the night together. For the moment it was hidden by a bank of high clouds, but the water shone and sparkled in the distance as the moonlight raced to catch up with us. In no time the cloud began to fray, and the moon emerged full and splendid. Once unfettered, its light revealed the silhouette of the *Oglebay's* tall stack and a long, curving line of smoke and steam that trailed behind us all the way back to the breakwall. There, at last, was visible proof that this was indeed a steamboat!

I watched as the smoke began to dissipate, an indication

that the engine was worked up. In minutes, the only visible clue to the force that was propelling us was the trail of steam from the atmospheric exhaust behind the stack, ever-present on all steamboats. From where I stood, that dancing wisp of steam seemed merely a benign vapor, a cloud, much as those overhead tonight. It was hard to believe that steam had the power to force the *Oglebay* through the water—even harder to believe that it had been the driving force of the Industrial Revolution.

From my vantage point, the *Oglebay*'s after end, with its smoking stack and deck abristle with machinery and pipes, appeared so detached that it could well have been another vessel following in our path. The only indication that the two were connected was that steady throbbing of the engine. I knew that back there, way astern, deep down in the engine room, was another place altogether, a frenetic world of fire and steam, hot grease and oil, immense flailing cranks, a world of myriad pumps and pipes of every description. The centerpiece, of course, was the engine, a triple-expansion behemoth, one of the last of its kind, driving us onward: the coal and men and steel that were the ship herself.

Here in the pilothouse, everything was as serene as the summer night. Ahead of us, the surface of the lake spread out all the way to where it met the sky beyond the edge of night. The glow of lights from other ports and cities on the Ohio coastline was still visible off to the southwest. Almost imperceptibly at first, I began to be aware of the lake beneath us, and of the *Oglebay*'s buoyancy. She was in her element now, no longer tied to a dock. Freed from the confines of the harbor, she responded by rising and falling gently with each swell, as if drawing deep breaths.

Bud, who had been standing—as all wheelsmen must when entering and leaving port—assumed a half-sitting position on a stool as he took up his vigil behind the wheel. Mark Kapa, the mate on watch, filled a Styrofoam cup with scalding black coffee from the never-empty pot and began calculating our "ETA" at Milwaukee by the light of a flashlight. Bob, who had not stopped pacing the pilothouse from the moment he arrived almost an hour ago, lit up a cigarette, settled back in his chair (the captain's chair on the starboard side of the pilothouse), put his feet up on the windowsill, and, looking at me, said, "Well, now you're really steamboating, Dave."

A little later, I went back aft for a "night lunch" in the mess. On my way forward again, I stopped by the rail to look out on the moonlit lake, hardly believing I was where I was.

"Not too many people see this."

I turned and saw Glenn Guy, one of the deckhands, who had materialized beside me. "We kind of take it all for

granted."

After a while he said, "It's a beautiful night."

We stood there in silence for some time before he spoke again: "There are no passenger steamers on the lakes anymore." Then, after a pause, he added, "We don't take any guests. You're the first passenger I remember we've had on board."

He knew I appreciated how lucky I was.

Afterward, I sat in the darkened pilothouse for what must have been fully three hours sipping coffee and soaking up the experience of being there, as a dry sponge takes up water. It was one of those rare occasions when I had the sense to appreciate the importance of something while it was happening. Finally, sleep began to overtake me—despite the coffee and my best efforts to keep it at bay. It was 2:30, and reluctantly I decided to turn in.

At first light I was back in the pilothouse again with the mate, John Biolchini. "You go through withdrawal when you get off the boat," he said with good humor. "You have nothing in common with those back home 'on the beach.' You're like a fifth wheel. Their lives have been going on without you. You feel out of place doing the simplest things like going to the store. On the boat you know the same twenty-six men. You smell each other's sweat every day. It's its own little world. Everything is the boat. Even when you're off watch and go to a bar in port, the conversation invariably goes back to the boat. It's there twenty-four hours a day, you don't ever escape it. It's like being in a voluntary prison. But it's a respectable job, especially among your coworkers. I like it—at this point in time. Can't see being married and having a family and doing it, though.

"I like change, dealing with the elements all the time. It's a challenge. It's you against the weather, the dock, the feeling that, come hell or high water, we'll get there."

He paused to pour himself a cup of coffee.

"These old self-unloaders like the *Oglebay* are *work*boats," he said with a smile. "But an ore boat, it's strictly routine, back and forth on the same route every six days.

"On the small ones, you go everywhere, all over the lakes. Big ports, little ports. These are real tramp steamers. We can go where the straight-deckers and the thousand-footers can't. We go up rivers and creeks, put out the boom and unload. You should see some of those places that pass for a dock. We've even tied up to a tree stump. Sometimes the boat is bigger than the river."

I told him that when I first began this book, I had discovered there was certain a mystique about straight-deckers, as if they were the only pure lakeboats—that all the others were philistines.

"Those used to be the 'glory boats.' They were in the gravy trade. The biggest, cleanest, most modern. They operated from port to port on more or less regular runs. In that way, they were like the transatlantic liners, except that a liner always goes on schedule, *period*, whereas the freighter waits until it is full.

"Then you had the unglamorous boats, the 'stone boats,' which were like workhorses compared to stallions, which since the turn of the century have been self-unloaders. They were the traditional tramp steamers," he explained, adding that all lake steamers technically are tramps because they are chartered to haul cargo from port to port.

He went on to say that boats like the *Oglebay*, and others like her, were too small to be viable for the straight-decker trade any longer, so they were converted to the self-unloader trade, calling at the smaller upriver ports—like Fairport, Bay City, and Ontonagon, where the 1,000-footers would run aground. "Bigness isn't everything."

I poured myself another cup of freshly brewed coffee from that never-empty pot in the pilothouse and brought up the subject of the art of maneuvering ships without tugs, which is the general rule on the lakes. Being from New York, where using tugs is common practice when docking and undocking a vessel, I had always marveled at the way lakeboats seemed to be able to work themselves in and out of almost any situation unassisted.

"It's the bow thruster. It's just like having a tug up there," John said without hesitation. Then he went on to explain: "The secret is to keep the speed down to 2 or 3 miles per hour. If you put on too much engine to kick the stern around, you will outrun the bow thruster. It's a matter of judicious use of the engine. You have to allow for the current and the wind, too, of course; try to get in a position where they work *for* you, rather than *against* you.

"If you do that all the time, you're one hell of a shiphandler. If you don't, you buy a lot of plates—hull plates. You bang 'em up so badly they have to be replaced."

This brought up the question of the degree of coordination required between the captain and the engineer of a steamboat.

"It's the lull period between engine changes that's critical. You want a guy down there who's quick on the throttle when the weather's bad and you ring the Chadburn."

I asked whether the mate ever used the Chadburn to signal the engineer.

"The Chadburn is basically the captain's tool. It's his prerogative to use it. The only time the mate operates engines is under the captain's orders, or in an emergency. The same is true for the bow thrusters. The captain must be in the pilothouse whenever the ship is in maneuvering waters. That's what he's paid for."

"Maneuvering waters?" I asked.

"Coming in and out of port. He must always be up here then."

"What about on the rivers?" I asked, remembering that the captain was always in the pilothouse during all the trips I had made through the rivers.

"Those are restricted waters," he explained. "In the rivers like the St. Clair, the St. Marys, it is *traditional* for the captain to be in the pilothouse. There are also restricted passages like Grey's Reef and Round Island. They're discretionary, too. If it's bad weather, if the mate's inexperienced, if there is a lot of traffic, then the captain may elect to come up. If it's clear and there's no traffic and he knows the mate knows what he is doing, then he may elect not to come up. Remember, the mate on watch is *in* charge. The old man is there to *take* charge."

"And what about calling the captain 'the old man'?" I asked. "Is it a derogatory term?"

"No, not at all. It's an affectionate term, not derogatory in any way. It's slang, though, so you wouldn't call him that to his face, but it is always used among the crew members, even by the first mate, who might be a relief captain on the same boat."

We talked more about about maneuvering, and I mentioned that the Kinsman boats employed a crew of men in a motorboat who used to go from place to place attaching cables at strategic points so the vessels could be winched around the bends in the Buffalo River.

"That was the way we had to do it before the days of the bow thruster. We relied a lot more on wires [cables] then.

"We still use a lot of wires when maneuvering, and it's up to the mate to coordinate the efforts on deck. You have to learn to anticipate the ship's movements. If you're too slow changing the wires—say, your timing is two or three minutes off—you can lose as much as 20 or 30 degrees. It's a real team effort. The mate is like a foreman. The captain tells him what he is going to do, how and where to place the wires, and the mate positions the deckhands accordingly.

"There is a lot of teamwork between the captain and the mate, too," he said with a smile that left no doubt he knew what he was talking about.

We are in the Detroit River and suddenly surrounded with boats of all kinds vying for a place in the shipping lanes. Most were pleasure craft of one sort or another that scudded away like frightened ducks as the *Oglebay* steamed by with implacable hauteur. There were lakers abroad as well: No fewer than twelve headed downbound passed us port to port. Four were steamers, albeit turbines: the *Arthur M. Anderson*, the *J. A. W. Iglehart*, the *Elmglen*, and the *J. L. Mauthe*. The newly renamed *Ernest R. Breech*, now the *Kinsman Independent*, one of the last American steamers built on the lakes, had been chasing our stern all morning. She finally caught up with us and left us far behind by the time we entered Lake St. Clair.

At 12:40 P.M., as we approached downtown Detroit, the mailboat, *J. W. Wescott*, raced out to meet us and pulled alongside. Mail and supplies were hauled up over the side, and bags of trash were handed back down. Not only is the *Wescott* the lifeline for the boat crews, it also happens to be the only vessel with its own zip code—48222.

Although the Detroit River seemed full to me this morning, it must have seemed like a ghost town compared to the way it was in the early 1900s, when a vessel passed Detroit on an average of once every six minutes during the height of the navigation season, and when it was said then to be the most heavily traveled waterway in the world. The tally amounted to some 38,000 passages from April to December, roughly ten times more than the Suez Canal saw in a full year. The river's total tonnage grossed more than 67,500,000 tons, an amount greater than that which entered all the major ports on the East Coast: New York, Baltimore, Philadelphia, Boston, Charleston, and Savannah.

During the course of the day, we passed a number of that hideous breed of new lake freighter, the so-called afterender.

"Just like a shoebox with an engine," Jim Roth, the third mate on the *Ayers*, had said disparagingly of them.

True. In essence, they are hardly ships at all, but merely immense motorized scows. Their design is dictated by efficiency, period. There is nothing reminiscent of maritime tradition in their appearance, inherently nothing nautical. They are absolutely square, with no "line" or sheer. In fact, all of them look as if they would be far more at home on dry land than afloat. The superstructure is piled up aft, as if it had been created from a set of Legos by a child playing on the living-room rug. The stack—for years one of the most prominent features in ship design—is no more than an afterthought.

The demise of the stack, or funnel, in vessels of recent vintage is one of the most conspicuous departures from traditional marine architecture. In the days of coal-burning vessels, and before the forced draft became commonplace, tall stacks were essential. They provided air to the furnaces and kept as much soot as possible from raining down upon the passengers. But the tall stacks were more than just a necessity, as borne out by the fact that dummy funnels often were used on a vessel where only one or two were actually functional. During the heyday of the steamship, the steamship companies and the traveling public alike seem to have decided that the more of them, and the taller, the better. Those great ocean liners with their towering funnels became not only synonymous with power and speed but also with national pride. Quite apart from the steamships' primary functions, they were ambassadors without portfolios, representing their countries in ports of call the world over. And they had yet another purpose, as well. To the fainthearted, a glance upward at those immense, smoke-belching funnels spoke of power and the implicit staunchness of the vessel to which they were about to entrust life and limb. It is said that this was especially true of immigrants, whose criterion for booking passage often was based solely on the number of stacks a vessel possessed.

Perhaps there is nothing we have ever built that so beautifully embodied the sense of adventure and excitement of travel as those grand old steamships with their towering funnels. I remembered them backing out into the Hudson, smoke pouring forth from their stacks, telling of the power needed for a crossing of the ocean and how I used to feel when the tugs turned them and when they began to head out to sea. How when they finally disappeared into that eternal gray that always seemed to be the color of the harbor, my imagination sailed away with them.

I mentioned to Bob the difference between the older ships with tall stacks and the newer vessels.

"You know, I asked for the *Oglebay*," he said. "These old boats are a lot better than some of the ones they build today. They may not have the speed, but they are real boats. Accountants didn't build steamboats then; shipowners built them.

"The new ships are like cars. Look at the fender of a 1950 Chevy, and then look at a 1990 GMC Pick Up. The '50 is solid, thick; the '90 is a piece of tin. The old hulls made of mild carbon steel were thicker than those of today's boats, which are made of high-tensile steel. It may be stronger, but the hull won't last as long as a thick one. Do you think the *Mesabi Miner* (a new 1,000-footer) will be around as long as the old *E. M. Ford*?"

He smiled and said, "Besides, the captain's quarters are better on the old boats. The new ones are so sterile. You know—no wood, very little brass."

It takes one hour twenty-five minutes at Shell Marine Service at Sarnia, Ontario, to fill the *Oglebay's* bunkers with 45,000 gallons of number 6 fuel oil—bunker "C," as it is called universally. It is remarkable how much fuel even a "small" boat like the *Oglebay* consumes. On average, she burns 5,848 gallons of oil a day, which, at the July 1990 price of 40.5 cents per gallon, means her fuel costs $2,252 per day. This is a drop in the bucket when compared to the thousand-footers, like the *Columbia Star*, which guzzle some 12,000 gallons of diesel fuel in twenty-four hours.

"Why do you take fuel in Canada?" I asked Bob.

"It's cheaper. Here it comes straight from the refinery to the boat."

While we were waiting, Bob told me a story about the first time the *Wolverine* stopped here to fuel up on her maiden trip through the rivers. After the bunkers were full, and when the time came to sign the bill for the oil, it was discovered that the *Wolverine* was not yet on Shell's list of charge customers. As luck would have it, the captain had a Shell credit card, so in order to avoid what would otherwise be a long delay while it was decided who would pay, he agreed to put the charges on his card. The *Wolverine* then went merrily on her way. About two weeks later, the captain's wife called the ship in desperation to ask him why there was a charge for $38,000 on his card.

"After three watches, you'd think we'd be out of the rivers," said Bob as we approached the Blue Water Bridge, the gateway to Lake Huron. Negotiating the St. Clair River coming upstream to the bridge is a tense operation under the best of circumstances, but tonight there are more than the usual problems. It has been fully twenty-four hours since we steamed out of Ashtabula, and we have been losing time all day. Ever since early afternoon, the engineers have been ministering to the *Oglebay*'s sore, old engine. The eccentrics on the intermediate cylinder are worn, and they need to be replaced. But in this day and age, eccentrics, like steam-engine parts in general, are almost as hard to come by as hen's teeth.

In the *Oglebay*'s case, there are only two choices: to have a new set made specially to order—and the patterns probably will cost more than the parts—or to cannibalize a pair from the engine of the *Robert C. Norton*, the *Oglebay*'s deactivated identical twin. Neither of these options is obviously much help tonight. To make matters more difficult, we are "hand steering," since the gyrocompass is not working. It was to have been repaired in Ashtabula, but the new parts were sent to Milwaukee instead, a full two days' steam away under the best of circumstances.

Then there is the weather. There is lightning everywhere! And there are storms all over the radar screen. The elements have been against us since early this morning. The fog was so heavy on the lower Detroit River that you could hardly see the end of the steering pole from the pilothouse. By midday, thunderstorms were building all around us. In the late afternoon, we were put under a tornado watch, which became a warning just as we arrived at the fuel dock.

"They can't seem to get more than 65 rpm out of the engine," Bob remarks after scanning the engine-speed indicator.

"Either the engineers are playing games with us or they must be worried tonight. Don't want to put too much strain on the engine. Well, at least we're not going backward," he says with a chuckle, lighting up another cigarette.

As we begin to make the final turn under the bridge, it seems we are scarcely moving against the current. The shoreline is barely creeping by, and I wonder if we even have enough speed to maintain steerageway. I can sense the wheelsman's nervousness as he responds to the mate's commands. The mate is new, and obviously nervous too. He keeps telling the wheelsman not to come too far to the right, so as not to end up on the Canadian shore. Bob sizes up the situation and finally says by way of gentle admonition, "Give your wheelsman a break," explaining that it is confusing to give too many commands too quickly.

I keep my eyes glued to the steering pole on the bow as we begin to negotiate the final bend. It is absolutely silent in the pilothouse. After what seems an eternity, the *Oglebay* straightens out, and we pass beneath the bridge right down the middle of the channel. I look at my watch; it's 11:37 P.M. I'm getting to be an old hand here, I thought to myself. This is my sixth trip under the bridge on a lake steamer this summer.

"Well, we're past buoys 1 and 2; that's a good omen," I hear Bob mutter to himself.

"How fast are we going?" the mate asks.

"About 8.8. Maybe they will wind her up once we're past buoys 7 and 8—I hope so. Never a dull moment on a steamboat, eh, Dave?" says Bob as he pours himself a cup of coffee and lights up yet another cigarette.

After we were safely past the buoys, heading out into Lake Huron I mentioned something to Bob about how much skill had been needed to maneuver the *Oglebay* through the channel under the bridge tonight.

He shrugged off the compliment. "The secret to running a river is to do the same thing over and over again. But when you're loaded and don't have horsepower, you can be screwed!"

I looked back as a flash of lightning illuminated the *Oglebay*'s afterhouse for an instant. How implacably calm this staunch old boat seemed, despite her ailing engine. There was something reassuring about that thin line of steam trailing away from her stack—stark white against the blackness of the night. The rain came in sheets, blown by gusts of wind. At times the lightning was so blinding it lit up the night like day, revealing the roiling, angry clouds and seas.

"I guess we'll have a working night tonight," said Bob succinctly.

I looked over at him and remembered being told that he wasn't a rough-weather man. Some captains have reputations for driving their ships and crews through terrible seas. Some get away with it and others "get caught with their pants down."

Bob kept his eye on the rpm indicator all the while he sipped his coffee, obviously not happy about what he saw. Finally he picked up the telephone and rang the engine room. I heard him ask Jack Fredericks, the chief engineer, "She's doing 10, chief. Is she maxed out?"

"O.K. Well, I guess there'll be no passing the *Crapo* this trip."

"Maybe we should call her for a tow," suggests the mate.

"I see the *Middletown* back there. We might call and ask her to 'check down' so she'd be going slow enough to give us a tow," said Bob with a chuckle. "Well, at least the wind is with us," he added. "Maybe we could tie the bedsheets together for sails."

I thought of what it was like in the engine room tonight. I remembered all the times I had been there myself, and what the men there had told me about what it was like to work below decks on a steamboat.

"Lots of fellows don't want to work on these boats," said Bill Phalen, one of the oilers, who has been sailing for thirty-five years.

"It's dirty, all that oil and water flying around. Besides, men going for engineer don't like to work over here because their license would be for limited horsepower. A fellow who works on the big ships can get a license that's good for any horsepower. But this is a better job than most," he assured me with a wide grin.

"It's a nice boat to pump out—pump the ballast tanks, you know. Equipment's kept up. It's simple and in good shape. That's what makes the oiler's job easier, when the deck crew keeps hollerin' to pump this tank or that; keep it in trim. These old steam pumps work good. The ones that were built in the fifties—pipes are all rusted out.

"My father sailed for Columbia twenty-five years. Got my seaman's card in 1955. Sailed salt water, sailed for PM [Pickands Mather]. Started out as a coal passer. Hand fired on the old ones, when 'most everyone was still shoveling by hand. Never been on a diesel."

Gene Lay, another oiler, said that working on the *Oglebay* was the "best darn oiling job on the lakes," and he wanted to stay on her as long as they ran her. "It's a good money boat, lots of overtime. You stay busy all the time. It takes me thirty minutes to make a good round—check everything, all the machinery, the engine, all the electric motors, the bearings, make sure nothing is hot. Just hope you don't lose a finger.

"I'm always going around with an oilcan. I like to move all the time. I don't like standing around. After they lay up the boats when I am back home, I sit around for a day or two, then I have to get up, wash dishes, anything to keep busy."

Terry Fisher, the son of Captain Howard Fisher of the *S. T. Crapo*, was the engineer on watch. I could imagine how incensed he was tonight because "his" engine wasn't up to par. I knew how much time he always spent adjusting this and that, listening to make sure it sounded right, and how concerned he was when it didn't. "I wouldn't say I was fond of it, but you walk around it a thousand times, you work on it, you become attached to it."

Earlier in the trip I had asked Jack, who has been the *Oglebay's* chief engineer ever since she was brought out of retirement in 1989, if hers was a good engine. He smiled, "I could have been on three different boats this spring, but I knew who was coming over here. I like the crew. That makes the difference."

I remembered my conversation last night with Dick McCarthy, the *Oglebay's* first assistant engineer, and wondered how he felt now.

"More things work on this boat than on a lot of them," he had said.

"Can I quote you?"

"It's the truth."

Those were words spoken with authority. McCarthy has been in engine rooms more than twenty-five years.

"I started sailing as a machinist's mate in the Coast Guard, spent forty-three months in the service, but didn't want to go to salt water. There's a better class of people out here. I wanted to go into the merchant marine, and U.S. Steel said we got ships and we need men, so I came over to the lakes. I was there from 1970 to 1986. When there was a steel strike, I came to Columbia."

We talked about the differences between being an engineer on a steamboat, and being one on a diesel, where on all of the newer, larger vessels, the engine is controlled by the captain.

"With pilothouse control, you just stand around. The captain does the whole thing.

"With a steamboat, it makes a difference who is in the engine room. The captain will do some things with one engineer he might not do with another. One may be slower than another. With a new engineer, the captain will avoid a quick 'full astern' situation."

It reminded me of a conversation I had had with another "first," Pete Stremel, in the engine room of the *Ayers* one night steaming down Lake Huron about his experience on the thousand-footer *Columbia Star*.

"On the *Star*, there was nothing to do but look busy," he said jokingly. "You would take a bunch of tools from the tool board, walk around, put them back, go to another board, take another bunch, and walk around some more. Over here, you don't have to try to look busy.

"Ninety-nine percent of the guys don't want to have anything to do with this. It's all bull work down here. I love it.

"It's like it says on the *Ayers* T-shirt the fellows had made: 'This is not just a job. It is an adventure—only a few good men are chosen.' "

The lights of the ancient *Nicolet*, downbound, hove into view, followed by those of the *Algocanyon*; in the distance, the silhouette of a saltwater boat was illuminated by the lightning. All three passed in turn, port to port, like perfect little models, glistening in the rain as if freshly painted. Then the lake was empty.

In time the bursts of rain became less frequent, the lightning less intense. Suddenly there was no wind, and an almost eerie calm began to settle on the night. The storm was dying. The clouds began to break apart, and the stars came out, one by one at first. Finally all was clear, and the newly risen moon revealed a sea of whitecaps spread over the surface of the lake.

The night now seemed washed clean by the storm. The air carried down the length of the lake from the boreal expanses of the Canadian wilderness was as pure as cool spring water.

I know of few places where the transition between man's world and God's is more abrupt than when passing beneath the Blue Water Bridge upbound into Lake Huron. All day, coming up through the river system past steel mills and refineries, we were suffused in industrial smog, at times so thick it was painful to breathe. Before us, a great expanse of lake and sky unfolded, stretching past the night, one can imagine, all the way to the edge of the universe. The distant lights of downbound ships on the interface between lake and sky are indistinguishable from the stars.

I stepped out on deck to be away from the smoke-filled atmosphere of the pilothouse and to breathe freely of the cool night air. There before me stretched not only the lake but also the expanse of *Oglebay*'s deck. I realized she was as much a part of the industrial world as the steel mills, refineries, and power plants that lined the riverbanks. And what of her cargo? Coal to generate electricity, to create acid rain, pollute the air,

kill the boreal forest in the bargain. But on this beautiful starlit night I had no wish to confront all those issues brought upon us by our technological society. This was a voyage and perhaps my last on a steamboat.

Today there are big changes afoot in the coal business. For years, Appalachian coal has been carried "upbound" on the lakes from ports such as Ashtabula. But environmental restrictions on the burning of high-sulfur coal, such as the *Oglebay* is laden tonight, means that ever more western low-sulfur coal will be shipped "downbound" from the Head-of-the-Lakes at Duluth and Superior in the holds of those immense 1,000-footers and others of their ilk.

I looked aft and saw the lights of man falling into perspective. Sarnia, that skeletal city of refineries on the other side of the bridge, now was but a diminishing red glow in the southern sky. Over it, the lightning of the receding storm still flashed as if to mark the site of a distant battlefield.

The watch changed at midnight. With it came a fresh round of coffee, and all the familiar pilothouse banter began anew.

"Tell you something," says Bob as he fills up his cup again, "this boat runs on bunker "C" and Hills Brothers."

Someone mentions the name "Crush Gordon," an old captain they all knew, and everyone begins to chuckle.

"Remember the time he ordered 100 gallons of floor wax to wax the sides of the holds so the cargo would slide more easily?"

Guffaws all 'round.

Then someone else chimes in with the story about the time he was stuck in the ice and ordered the crew to pour rock salt all around the boat to melt it.

"You're not serious?" I ask incredulously, having heard some pretty good yarns before.

"Absolutely," everyone assures me. "It's a story told all over the lakes."

"Dave, did you ever hear about standing 'spark watch'?"

"No."

"Well, when a new deckhand would come on board an old coal burner, the guys would tell him to keep looking for the sparks coming out of the stack, (which they always did) and as soon as he saw any to go find the captain right away, even if he was sleeping and wake him up."

"How about you, cap'n? That ever happen to you?"

"No, but I've been wakened for some pretty strange reasons."

"Remember how they used to tell a new hand to ask the bo's'n for the keys so he could give them to the mate to open the lock when going through the Soo Locks?"

Everyone chuckles.

Soon the conversation turns to fishing, as it usually does, and everyone begins swapping tall tales of another sort.

Howard Foris, the *Oglebay*'s wiper/gateman, stopped by to tell Bob something and stayed long enough for a cup of coffee. I had been told that he came from a long line of lake men, so I asked him about his life on the boats.

"Since 1941, someone in the immediate family has always worked for Columbia. Whole family comes from Ashland, Wisconsin. In my dad's family, there were five uncles who sailed with Columbia and one for Boland, and one on salt water. My mother always said if your Uncle John had been a plumber, you all would have been plumbers. Would have followed the leader like bloody sheep.

"I've been with Columbia for twenty-five years, my dad had twenty-six, an uncle had thirty, another uncle was captain thirty-eight years. Had another who retired as first mate in 1967 after twenty years. Had a cousin, too, who quit after about fifteen years. That's 154 man years so far!" he said with a look of unmistakable pride.

I asked him whether he had any children.

He replied that he had two girls, both of whom vow they will never marry a sailor: "Don't want to be 'steamboat widows.'"

A little after three, Bob yawns and says he "figures it's time to get a little sleep. Call me if you need me." He gets up, stretches, and heads for the door on the starboard side. On the way out, he pauses and calls to me, "Dave, you can use my chair. Put your feet up and watch the sunrise. Can't say you've really been steamboating till you have. It's a beautiful sight."

The last time I saw the *Oglebay*, I was standing at the harbor mouth in Milwaukee late one frigid December afternoon. It was nearly sunset as I watched her steam away toward the horizon. This was her last trip my way for the season. It was nearly time for winter lay-up—one week, two at most, and the *Oglebay* and the *Ayers*, too, would be done for the year. And these days, whenever a steamboat is laid up, there is always a question of whether it will ever run again. Who could tell whether she would steam into port next spring all freshly painted and sparkling after fitting-out? Perhaps this would be the last chance to see her. Steamboats are biologically extinct. Once the few remaining individuals are gone, there will be no more. This was 1990, ten years before the end of the twentieth century, deep into an age far different from the *Oglebay*'s.

I took one more last look before I turned to go. She was still there, as if preserved in amber, as if there would always be steamboats out there, as there have been for as long as I can remember. How empty the lakes, and less interesting the world, will be without the likes of the *Oglebay*. How many places, how many more times, I thought, would one be able to stand at the mouth of a harbor and contemplate the sight of a steamer on the horizon? How hard to imagine the world without steam, I thought, as I settled behind the wheel of my car for the drive home.

CHAPTER 4

"Guess I'll take her to her grave," said Captain Dietlin of the *Irvin L. Clymer* over lunch one hot August day while we were loading a cargo of salt in Cleveland.

"Hate to see her go, but they say it'll cost $7,000,000 just to fix up the cargo holds. I'd rather see $7,000,000 in my pocket than in the hold," said the steward with a chuckle as he cleared the table.

"Be a shame if they scrapped her. She's the 'Queen of the Lakes,' that's for sure," said the mate as he got up to go. "Everyone wants to work on her—late fitting-out, early lay-up. We treat her kindly, though. Don't take her out in rough weather. Her hull's O.K., but she's old. Wouldn't want to find out just how old. Right, cap'n?"

I asked where her last trip might be.

"We might take her to Montreal so they can make razor blades out of her," Captain Dietlin replied. "Many old boats go out that way. They tow a lot overseas to be scrapped, too." He paused: "Quite a few are lost before they ever get there; sunk in storms on the ocean. Maybe it'll be to Fraser's in Superior. Maybe back home to Duluth. Nobody knows. They might even lay her up in Calcite, just in case they need her again. That's where she was always laid up every winter."

After lunch, I stopped to watch the white stream of salt pouring into the hold. Salt, the kiss of death for metal. How ironic that a ship that has lasted so many years because she sailed on the sweetwater sea should be eaten out from within by the salt that eventually destroys all ocean vessels from without.

"Road salt to rust out your car," said Wayne Coulsen, the third mate, laughing. "We load salt down here to eat the fenders off cars, then bring back taconite pellets to make the steel to build new fenders."

"She's a mighty fine old vessel. Supported many a family over the years," Wheelsman Wayne Selke said to me later while I was photographing his room.

The *Clymer's* long life began as hull number 718 on the ways of the American Shipbuilding Company in Lorain, Ohio. She was built as a boom-type self-unloader—one of the first vessels designed as such—for the Bradley Transportation Line, part of the Michigan Limestone & Chemical Company of Rogers City, Michigan. She made her maiden voyage on June 10, 1917, as the *Carl D. Bradley* and sailed away to Calcite to become part of that illustrious fleet of gray-hulled limestone boats known the lakes over. Like most of the older "stone boats," she was smaller than the ore carriers. Her overall dimensions were 552 feet by 60 feet by 32 feet. As originally built, she was equipped with a 2,100-horsepower, three-cylinder, triple-expansion reciprocating engine—similar to most in use on the lakes at the time—and three single-ended Scotch (firetube) boilers.

In 1927, when the new and ill-fated fleet flagship *Carl D. Bradley*—lost in 1958—was abuilding, she was renamed the *John G. Munson*. In 1943, her old Scotch boilers were replaced with Foster-Wheeler Type-D watertube boilers. At the same time, Hoffman Spreader stokers were installed on all furnaces.

In 1951, her name was changed for the third and final time. In that year, as the vessel that was to become the present *John G. Munson* was being built, she became the *Irvin L. Clymer*. At the beginning of the 1954 shipping season, she sailed out of Calcite sporting a new 4,000-horsepower General Electric single-rotor steam turbine, which had replaced her original old triple.

"Is there any kind of ceremony when you bring her into port for the last time?" I asked Captain Dietlin at the end of October when I saw him in Milwaukee on the *Clymer's* next-to-last trip.

"No. We just lock her up and go home."

I remembered the farewells in New York Harbor, when fireboats sprayed water in the air and all the vessels in the harbor blew their whistles in a final salute.

Captain Dietlin did, indeed, sail the old "Queen of the Lakes," as the *Clymer* was called by many, to her grave. I wasn't on hand for her last departure, but from one who was, I understand it was a beautiful, cloudless fall afternoon when she steamed out of Milwaukee onto the clear blue waters of Lake Michigan. I can see her in my mind's eye—such occasions are graven in my memory.

The *Clymer* steamed over the horizon that afternoon bound for Calcite, next to Rogers City. On November 3, 1990, she arrived at the Michigan Limestone Company's docks, where her hold was loaded with limestone, the cargo she had been built to carry, and filled her coal bunkers for the last time. Then she bade a final farewell to her old homeport and steamed north to Cedarville, on Michigan's Upper Peninsula. There she was filled to capacity with more stone. Finally she turned and headed for the "Soo," bound for the Head-of-the-Lakes with her last cargo—11,091 net tons of flux pellet stone. She arrived in Duluth on November 7 and tied up at Hallet dock number 5.

Today she is at Fraser's Shipyard in Superior, laid up, deactivated, awaiting a more favorable scrap market.

The *Clymer's* passing didn't go entirely unnoticed. According to Ilona Mason, one of the fleet's dispatchers in Duluth, who had kept me informed of the *Clymer's* whereabouts all season, "there wasn't a dry eye in town when she steamed under the bridge."

My love of steam engines has always kept me just one step ahead of the wrecking ball. I have been on hand for the final trips of so many locomotives and boats that the singular events themselves have become a mélange of farewells. Having often traveled thousands of miles to find steamboats, it is ironic to have found some of the last survivors in my own backyard.

A few years ago, I found myself on the beach at Waukegan, Illinois, looking out to "sea" for the first sign of the *J. B. Ford*, one of the lakes' most ancient denizens. I paced back and forth across the sand for an hour or more, setting flocks of gulls and nesting terns to flight as I scanned the horizon. Suddenly, where there had been nothing a moment before, it was there, as if by magic, an apparition suspended between water and sky. At that moment, I could as well have been on the Baltic, or the South China Sea—anyplace but at Waukegan, in the depths of the American heartland, with cornfields and the prairie at my back. From all appearances, the *Ford* might as easily have been steaming over the crest of the sea from afar, confirming the roundness of the earth—not just from "St. Joe" in Michigan, a mere seven hours across the lake.

The *Ford* was launched in 1904, with an engine made the year before. By many strokes of good fortune, and with a good measure of loving care bestowed upon her, she had outlasted virtually all of her contemporaries. A humble cement carrier; a former transporter of iron ore; a venerable, hardy old work-boat. She was almost the only vessel on the lakes with the hallmarks of a true steamer, and, deep within the hold, a staunch old triple moving up and down, up and down, up and down, still keeping stride.

Almost everything else about the *Ford's* era had crumbled away. She was virtually alone on the water now, approaching not only Waukegan but also the end of nearly a century of work. The *Ford* had sailed the Great Lakes before the golden age of steamships—even before the *Mauretania*, the *Titanic*. She was laying down a pall of smoke over the lakes at the same time immense express liners on the North Atlantic were pouring coal smoke from their funnels while they vied with one another for the coveted Blue Riband. She was hauling iron ore from the Mesabi Range during World War I when battleships of the Royal Navy were steaming toward Jutland, and again in World War II when our own fleet was steaming toward the Coral Sea.

The *Ford* was born the *Edwin F. Holmes* in the most prosaic of circumstances in the middle of middle America, in Lorain,

Ohio—about as far away from the rest of the world as the rest of the world could imagine. She was an ore boat made of steel, from a city made by steel itself. The *Ford*, ex-*Holmes*, ex-*E. C. Collins*, was a worker plain and simple, destined to fill her holds with bulk stuff—iron ore, wheat, and now cement—destined to spend a life on the inland seas bound for places like Muskegon, Alpena, and Waukegan.

As I contemplated the *Ford's* unhurried progress, the old boat seemed so distant that I kept having to convince myself it was really there. I saw two puffs of steam drift lazily away from her funnel, and a few seconds later, I heard the sound of the whistle. Suddenly I was overcome by the realization that in just a few years, these old boats probably would be gone for good.

Until a few years ago, if you wanted to find old lake steamers, one of the best places to look was Buffalo. Buffalo was the bailiwick of the quintessential straight-decker, the last of the classic "600-footers." In season, you could almost always see a telltale line of steam trailing from the stack of an old laker somewhere along the Buffalo River. If your curiosity was aroused by such things, a little exploration of the riverfront would probably reveal one of the venerable steamers of the Kinsman Lines lurking among the grain elevators.

The stock-in-trade of the Steinbrenner family's Kinsman Marine Transit Company has been the transport of grain from the Head-of-the-Lakes to Buffalo—traditionally one of the more profitable trade routes. However, with the opening of the Saint Lawrence Seaway in 1953, the traffic patterns on the lakes changed forever. For many a shipowner and port on the American side of the lakes, the seaway turned out to be as much of a "grand delusion" as its detractors had always claimed. Half of the grain traffic that had been carried in U.S. vessels was siphoned away by the "salties" (foreign-flag freighters), which transported it directly overseas from lake ports, and Canadian vessels that carried it far down the St. Lawrence, where it was off-loaded onto oceangoing freighters.

Buffalo in particular suffered. The harbor that once rivaled Liverpool began to wither. However, even though its role as a grain port and milling center was greatly diminished, and most of its mills and grain elevators stand unused, there is still enough business to keep three American-flag vessels dedicated to this trade. Interlake Steamship Company's *J. L. Mauthe* and two Kinsman boats, as well as an occasional Canadian vessel, still tie up beside the elevators, where their cargo is dipped and scooped out of their holds in basically the same way it has been done for 150 years.

The Kinsman Lines has always been known for its collection of vintage straight-deck bulkers. All of these had been "pre-driven," to borrow a term from the used-car dealers' lexicon. Many a ship ended its career under the Kinsman flag, after its former owners had decided it was no longer economical to maintain. Prior to 1989, the backbone of its fleet consisted of hand-me-down vessels from U.S. Steel's once vast flotilla of 600-footers. All were coal burners, and were still powered by their original three-cylinder, triple-expansion engines.

For years the lake ports were filled with all manner of mothballed vessels that had many years of life left in their hulls. So long as there was a plentiful supply of these, the Kinsman Lines had no trouble finding boats. When they were worn out, the company sent them to the ship breakers to be "turned into razor blades," and then replenished their stock from various sources around the lakes. However, today there are no more idle old lakeboats waiting for a buyer, virtually all have been scrapped.

Today the Kinsman fleet is a far cry from the one I first knew fifteen years ago. It consists of two active vessels, both of which are powered by steam turbines—the first in the company's history. The present Kinsman Independent, (the third boat of that name), formerly the Ernest R. Breech, was built in 1952 as the Charles L. Hutchinson. She was purchased from Ford Motor Company's Rouge Steel Company in 1988. The line's other vessel, the Kinsman Enterprise has had a long and illustrious career. As the ex-Harry Coulby, for years she was the flagship of the Interlake Steamship Company's fleet. On July 1, 1940, she broke all previous records by carrying the largest cargo of iron ore on the lakes—16,067 tons—an honor she was to claim again and again over the next fifteen years. (By comparison, a thousand-footer can carry nearly 70,000 tons.) On the lakes, record tonnage is an accolade akin to the coveted Blue Riband awarded to ships that made the fastest passage across the North Atlantic.

The Coulby was built as hull number 798 at the American Shipbuilding Company yard in Lorain, Ohio. She made her maiden voyage on September 10, 1927, two months before the S. T. Crapo was launched. During winter lay-up in 1957, her original triple-expansion engine was replaced with a 5,000-horsepower deLaval cross-compound steam turbine. At the same time, she was reboiled with oil-fired watertube boilers. In 1981, she was laid up, inactive, and finally put up for sale. After an eight-year hiatus, she reentered service as the Kinsman Enterprise in June 1989.

The grand old Kinsman Independent (2) that I knew so well is gone. Her last active season was 1987. Formerly U.S. Steel's Pittsburgh Steamship Division's 600-footer Richard V. Lindabury, she was built as hull number 783 at the American Shipbuilding Company yard in Lorain, Ohio, in 1923. Other than being reboiled and equipped with stokers in April 1956, she remained virtually unchanged all her life and continued to be powered by her original 2,200-horsepower triple until June 1988, when she was sold for scrap to the Marine Salvage Company of Port Colborne, Ontario.

The Merle M. McCurdy was another alumnus of Pittsburgh Steamship Division's 600-foot class. She was built as hull number 75 on the ways of the Great Lakes Engineering Works at Ecorse, Michigan, and was launched as the William B. Dickson in 1910. As such, she spent most of her life dutifully hauling cargoes of iron ore down from Lake Superior. After thirty-four years' service, she was reboiled and equipped with Stokers in 1944. In 1969, the Kinsman Lines bought her and renamed her. The McCurdy, incidentally, was the first boat on the lakes to be named for a black American, who was the U.S. attorney for the Northern District of Ohio. For the next eighteen years, she plied the lakes between Duluth and Superior and Buffalo, but now the holds of the former ore carrier were loaded with prairie wheat. Time finally caught up with the McCurdy in her seventy-seventh year. She was sold for scrap in 1987.

Unquestionably, one of the grand ships on the lakes is the Henry Steinbrenner, ex-William A. McGonagle. Today she is the last example of an unmodified standard 600-foot bulk freighter in existence. Like her nearly identical sister, the Kinsman Independent, ex-Lindabury, she can trace her lineage straight back to the J. Pierpont Morgan of 1906.

Until 1986, the Steinbrenner sailed under her original name—first as part of U.S. Steel's Pittsburgh Steamship fleet of vessels, and after December 7, 1978, for Kinsman Lines. Like the McCurdy, she began life at the Great Lakes Engineering Works in Ecorse. Designated hull number 154 until she was christened, the McGonagle made her maiden voyage on July 26, 1916, from Detroit to Duluth. There she entered the iron-ore trade, where she was destined to spend most of an uneventful life before becoming a hauler of grain. It seems that the only significant modifications to her machinery were the addition of mechanical stokers. She, too, like the first and second "K. I." and the McCurdy, was always powered by her original triple.

That ancient denizen of the lakes, the J. B. Ford, steams no more. She was taken out of service at the end of the 1985 shipping season. Today she is a cement barge moored at the LaFarge Corporation's plant on the Calumet River in South Chicago. Her boilers are cold, her old engine stilled, her once-glistening rods and cranks encased in layers of congealed oil.

That old "paradise for lovers of steam," the *McGonagle*, now the *Henry Steinbrenner*, was taken out of service at the end of the 1989 shipping season. Since December of that year she has been laid up inactive at Toledo. The *J. Burton Ayers* was laid up at the "Frog Pond" in Toledo in December 1990. She is there today, awaiting an uncertain fate. The *Crispin Oglebay*, was brought out on April 20, 1991, with the expectation of a full season of hard work ahead. But there was not enough business. She was laid up on May 29, with little hope of ever returning to service.

It is improbable that either the *Ayers* or the *Oglebay* will ever steam again, and according to the Oglebay Norton, not as part of its fleet. Their certificates expire in 1994 and it seems certain that they will be put up for sale at that time, either for conversion into barges, or for scrap. There is another reason, too, that conspires against their survival. In December 1990, Oglebay Norton purchased two newer and far more efficient vessels from Bethlehem Steel—the 1,000-foot *Lewis Wilson Foy*, renamed the *Oglebay Norton*, and the 698-foot *Sparrow's Point*, renamed the *Buckeye*, which increased its fleet capacity by 26 percent.

Currently, the only active steam-powered Maritime-class vessel is the *Willowglen*, owned by the Canadian firm Parrish & Heimbecker Ltd. The *Willowglen* has the further distinction of being one of two Canadian steam vessels on the Great Lakes to be powered by reciprocating engines. The other is ULS Corporation's *James Norris*, which was built in 1952 and is still powered by her original Skinner 4,800-horsepower unaflow. Except for the fact that the *Willowglen* never was converted to a self-unloader, she is virtually identical to the *Crispin Oglebay*. Formerly Bethlehem Steel Corporation's *Lehigh*, she was built at the Great Lakes Engineering Works yard at River Rouge, Michigan, and made her maiden voyage on November 1, 1943. Aside from the *Willowglen*, there are only two other Maritime-class boats still in service: Erie Sand Steamship Company's *Richard Reiss*, which was converted to diesel power in 1976, and USS Great Lakes Fleet's *George A. Sloan*, which was dieselized in 1985.

Of all the steamboats pictured in this book, only three can look forward to a reasonably long and productive life: the *Kinsman Enterprise* and the *John G. Munson* (both powered by turbines), and the *Medusa Challenger*, the last American laker to be powered by a unaflow. Their engines are still efficient, their hulls sound. If there is cargo for them to haul, there is little doubt that they, and the remaining turbine-powered lakers, will be steaming in and out of port for some time to come.

The future of the classic old steamers—the heart and soul of this book—is a different matter altogether. Only the *S. T.* *Crapo* is in service at this time.

The *Crapo's* future as a vessel seems assured for a long time—but perhaps not as a steamboat. For several years, plans have been in place to dieselize her. Although her engine is beautifully maintained, the fact that her boilers are old (and that she is coal fired) conspires against her being a steamer in the long run. Happily, her owner Inland Lakes Management plans to keep her as she is at least through the 1993 season.

Ironically, of all old lakers, the one that has the best chance for survival as a steamboat is the most ancient of them all—the *E. M. Ford*, another vessel in Inland Lakes' remarkable fleet of steamers.

The *E. M. Ford* began life in the most prosaic of circumstances. She was laid down as Steamer number 30 on the ways of Ohio's Cleveland Shipbuilding Company in February 1898, the same month the battleship *Maine* blew up in Havana Harbor. She was launched on May 25 of the same year, about the time Teddy Roosevelt and the Rough Riders were charging up San Juan Hill. She was christened the *Presque Isle* in July of that year.

For the next fifty-seven years, the *Presque Isle* steamed back and forth over the lakes carrying iron ore from the ranges of Michigan's Upper Peninsula to the blast furnaces of Cleveland for her owners, the Presque Isle Transportation Company, a subsidiary of the Cleveland Cliffs Steamship Company. In this role she joined the ranks of hundreds of other similar vessels that collectively formed the greatest inland transportation system the world has ever known. By 1955, however, her 428-foot length was considered small compared with other boats in the ore trade. Her owners deemed she was no longer economical to operate, and they put her up for sale. Given her size and age, it seemed as if her long, albeit uneventful, life had come to an end, and that she would be scrapped. But the old boat was to prove she had almost as many lives as a cat. She was bought by the Huron Cement Company and converted into a self-unloading cement carrier. She was rechristened the *E. M. Ford*, in honor of Huron Cement's chairman, and returned to service in 1956.

However mundane her previous existence, her new name and trade were to bring her much notoriety. On her very first voyage, she rammed and sank the steamer *A. M. Byers* in the St. Clair River. The *Ford* herself suffered considerable damage, which required replacing her bow. During the next few years, she underwent several face-lifts. In 1957, her forward cabins and pilothouse were replaced by a disproportionally high superstructure. In 1960, when the after cabins were replaced, the *Ford's* metamorphosis was complete: She looked nothing like the erstwhile *Presque Isle*. In 1975, her coal-fired boilers were converted to oil and the engine room was automated.

On Christmas Eve 1979, it seemed as if her time finally had come. While laid up at Jones Island in Milwaukee, one of those infamous winter gales blew up on Lake Michigan. Despite the fact that the *Ford* appeared to be moored securely, the wind and seas proved too great to withstand. The lines parted and the hapless *Ford* was driven against an adjacent pier and seawall, where she sank on Christmas Day. But Lady Luck still favored the venerable old boat. Divers quickly determined that she was salvageable, and the decision was made to have her towed to Sturgeon Bay, Wisconsin, for repairs. There was one small problem, however: The *Ford* was loaded with 5,580 tons of cement. The fact that it had set to a thickness of only 3 or 4 feet was the ship's salvation. Nonetheless, all of it had to be removed, a task that was accomplished largely by men with picks, shovels, and jackhammers. The reconditioning and overhauling of the vessel's machinery, including the entire electrical system, was accomplished by July 1980, and on August 7, the *E. M. Ford* steamed forth once again.

There is a footnote to the *Ford's* saga. Had the sinking occurred in salt water, the ending would have been very different. The machinery would have been too badly corroded by the time it was refloated to have been salvageable.

During the summer of 1991, the *Ford* sailed to Fraser's Shipyard at Superior for her five-year inspection and was certified to run until 1996, when she will be ninety-eight years old. However, her future is not as bright as it would seem. On June 6, 1991, Inland Lakes Management's latest acquisition, the turbine-powered steamer *Alpena*, went into service. Formerly the USS Great Lakes fleet's *Leon Fraser*, the *Alpena* is, incidentally, the last surviving member of the Pittsburgh Steamship class of "super ships" built in 1942. She is a classic in her own right, having all the lines of a true laker. It is very possible that she could well be the very last of the great tall-stacked, counter-sterned steamers on the lakes. With the arrival of the *Alpena*, the *Ford* was withdrawn from regular

service. She will be used now as a standby vessel in the event that one of the company's four other vessels is in need of repair or inspection, or if the cement trade warrants another boat. Presently she is being used for cement storage at Green Bay, Wisconsin. However, there are no plans afoot at this time to dispose of this remarkable old steamer. Should the *Ford* be active in 1998, she will be 100 years old. If she is still in service two years later, she—the oldest laker of them all—could very possibly be the last merchant ship powered by reciprocating engines in North America (if not the world) at the beginning of the twenty-first century.

The *Ford's* longevity is her primary claim to fame. Her appearance has been drastically altered over the years, so she now bears little resemblance to the ship that once was the *Presque Isle*. Her engine, however, is the same as the day it was built in 1897. It is a masterpiece—unquestionably one of the most perfect examples of nineteenth-century marine technology in existence. It also is the only true quadruple-expansion engine in service in North America—perhaps the world— and reputedly is the only known engine to employ Joy valve gear, a novel system of admitting steam, which is used on all but the *Ford's* low-pressure cylinder.

Quite apart from its other distinctions, it also happens to be a most beautiful machine.

That this creation of the nineteenth century might actually steam into the twenty-first is quite remarkable given the useful life of most vessels. More significant is the fact that *any* of these old lakers, whose fortunes I have followed so closely during the past few years, were at work in the last decade of the twentieth century. These are not museum pieces. Quite the contrary. They have been in everyday use hauling the same kind of cargoes for which they were designed far longer than any steam vessels on this continent. Collectively, these unglamorous old boats are among the purest and very best examples of the technology that provided the basis for the Industrial Revolution. When they are gone, the age of steam transportation will have come to an end in America. We shall not see "such ships as these again."

Steamer WILLIAM A. MCGONAGLE, *Buffalo, New York.*

Steamer J. BURTON AYERS *and Steamer* PAUL H. CARNAHAN *at Burlington Northern Railway,*
Allouez ore docks, Superior, Wisconsin.

Steamer KINSMAN INDEPENDENT, *Superior, Wisconsin.*

Steamer CRISPIN OGLEBAY, *Milwaukee, Wisconsin.*

Steamer J. BURTON AYERS, *South Chicago, Illinois.*

Steamer IRVIN L. CLYMER, *Milwaukee, Wisconsin.*

Steamer IRVIN L. CLYMER, *Calcite, Michigan.*

Steamer J. BURTON AYERS. *View of bow showing A-frame of self-unloading mechanism. South Chicago, Illinois.*

Detail of hull, ore carrier, USS Great Lakes Fleet, Duluth, Minnesota.

Steamer J. BURTON AYERS *loading coal at KCBX Corporation dock, South Chicago, Illinois.*

Steamer CRISPIN OGLEBAY *loading coal at Norfolk Southern Railway dock, Sandusky, Ohio.*

Steamer CRISPIN OGLEBAY, *Cleveland, Ohio.*

Steamer J. BURTON AYERS *loading taconite pellets at Allouez ore docks, Superior, Wisconsin.*

Steamer J. BURTON AYERS *loading taconite pellets at Allouez ore docks, Superior, Wisconsin.*

Duluth, Missabe & Iron Range Railroad ore dock, Duluth, Minnesota.

Steamer WILLIAM A. MCGONAGLE *in Buffalo River, Buffalo, New York.*

Steamer E. M. FORD *at LaFarge Corporation cement plant, Alpena, Michigan.*

Steamer WILLIAM A. MCGONAGLE, *Buffalo, New York.*

Steamer KINSMAN INDEPENDENT *loading at grain elevator, Superior, Wisconsin.*

Steamer KINSMAN INDEPENDENT, *Duluth, Minnesota.*

View of "straight-decker" WILLIAM A. MCGONAGLE, *showing hatch covers, Buffalo, New York.*

Steamer WILLIAM A. MCGONAGLE *at General Mills, Buffalo, New York.*

Steamer IRVIN L. CLYMER, *Milwaukee, Wisconsin.*

Steamer J. B. FORD *in Lake Michigan off Waukegan, Illinois.*

Steamer J. B. FORD *in Lake Michigan off Waukegan, Illinois.*

Steamer S. T. CRAPO *departing Waukegan, Illinois.*

Steamer CRISPIN OGLEBAY *departing Sandusky, Ohio.*

Stack, Steamer CRISPIN OGLEBAY.

Steamer CRISPIN OGLEBAY, *view of boat deck, showing engine-room ventilator cowls and base of stack.*

Steam winch, Steamer CRISPIN OGLEBAY.

Pilothouse, Steamer IRVIN L. CLYMER.

Pilothouse, chart table, Steamer KINSMAN INDEPENDENT.

Steamer S. T. CRAPO *on Lake Michigan, view looking aft from Texas deck.*

Steamer S. T. CRAPO *on* Lake Michigan, *view of bow and steering pole from pilothouse.*

Steamer S. T. CRAPO *on Lake Michigan, view past stateroom door, looking forward.*

"Rec" room, Steamer S. T. CRAPO.

Ship's office, Steamer S. T. CRAPO.

Guest stateroom, Steamer S. T. CRAPO.

Third mate's cabin, Steamer S. T. CRAPO.

Watchman's cabin, Steamer IRVIN L. CLYMER.

Mess, Steamer IRVIN L. CLYMER.

Galley, Steamer HENRY STEINBRENNER (*ex*-WILLIAM A. MCGONAGLE).

Galley, Steamer S. T. CRAPO.

Firehold, Steamer KINSMAN INDEPENDENT.

Firehold, Steamer WILLIAM A. MCGONAGLE.

Firehold, Steamer IRVIN L. CLYMER.

Firehold, Steamer S. T. CRAPO.

Rodney Ruell, fireman, cleaning fires, Steamer S. T. CRAPO.

Rodney Ruell, fireman, cleaning fires, Steamer S. T. CRAPO.

Rodney Ruell, fireman, Steamer S. T. CRAPO.

Bob Powell, fireman, Steamer WILLIAM A. MC GONAGLE.

Walter M. Brown, stokerman, Steamer IRVIN L. CLYMER.

Paul Wouri, fireman, Steamer WILLIAM A. MCGONAGLE.

Joe McKay, fireman, Steamer S. T. CRAPO.

Michael Quaine, stokerman, Steamer IRVIN L. CLYMER.

Engine room, Steamer S. T. CRAPO, *looking toward boiler room.*

Leonard Werda, chief engineer, Steamer S. T. CRAPO.

Engine room, Steamer IRVIN L. CLYMER, *showing desk and Chadburn.*

Douglas Monk, third assistant engineer, Steamer IRVIN L. CLYMER.

Keith McHugh, first assistant engineer, Steamer KINSMAN ENTERPRISE.

Engine room, Steamer KINSMAN ENTERPRISE.

Detail of quadruple-expansion engine, Steamer E. M. FORD.

James Wheatley, third assistant engineer, Steamer E. M. FORD.

View of quadruple-expansion engine from throttle deck, Steamer E. M. FORD.

End view of triple-expansion engine of Steamer CRISPIN OGLEBAY, *showing Stephenson linkage.*

Detail of connecting rods and cranks, Lenz Standard Marine Engine, Steamer J. BURTON AYERS.

End view of triple-expansion engine from crank deck of Steamer CRISPIN OGLEBAY.

Bill Phalen, oiler, Steamer CRISPIN OGLEBAY.

Triple expansion engine, low-pressure cylinder, Steamer WILLIAM A. MC GONAGLE.

Engine room, Steamer J. BURTON AYERS. *View along top of engine.*

Engine room, Steamer IRVIN L. CLYMER.

Dick McCarthy, first assistant engineer, Steamer CRISPIN OGLEBAY.

Detail of triple-expansion engine, throttle deck, Steamer CRISPIN OGLEBAY.

Pete Stremel, first assistant engineer, Steamer J. BURTON AYERS.

Engine controls, Lenz Standard Marine Engine, Steamer J. BURTON AYERS.

Steering engine, Steamer S. T. CRAPO.

Instrument board, engine room, Steamer J. B. FORD.

Ballast pump, engine room, Steamer J. BURTON AYERS.

Engine room, Steamer KINSMAN ENTERPRISE.

View of tunnel showing self-unloading conveyor mechanism, Steamer J. BURTON AYERS.

Port-side crew tunnel, Steamer J. BURTON AYERS.

Cargo hold, Steamer CRISPIN OGLEBAY.

Cleaning hold, Steamer CRISPIN OGLEBAY.

Cleaning hold, Steamer CRISPIN OGLEBAY.

Scoopers in hold of Steamer WILLIAM A. MCGONAGLE, *Buffalo, New York.*

Scoopers in hold of Steamer HENRY STEINBRENNER (*ex-*WILLIAM A. MCGONAGLE), *Buffalo, New York.*

Scooper in hold of Steamer WILLIAM A. MCGONAGLE, *Buffalo, New York.*

Captain Al Ritteman, Steamer WILLIAM A. MCGONAGLE.

Captain Edward ("Bud") Tambourski, Steamer J. BURTON AYERS.

Howard Foris, wiper/gateman, Steamer CRISPIN OGLEBAY.

Edward Thuning, wiper/gateman, Steamer CRISPIN OGLEBAY.

Ron Millard, deckhand, Steamer CRISPIN OGLEBAY.

Steve Schmidt, deckhand, Steamer J. BURTON AYERS.

Right: Steamer MEDUSA CHALLENGER. *Left: Hull number 3, ex-Steamer* STEELTON. *Lake Calumet, Chicago, Illinois.*

Steamer IRVIN L. CLYMER, *Milwaukee, Wisconsin.*

———

Unloading cement clinker from Steamer KINSMAN INDEPENDENT, *Superior, Wisconsin.*

Steamer KINSMAN INDEPENDENT, *Superior, Wisconsin.*

Steamer IRVIN L. CLYMER *passing under Conrail Bridge, Cleveland, Ohio.*

———

142

Steamer IRVIN L. CLYMER *unloading salt, Milwaukee, Wisconsin.*

Steamer E. M. FORD *loading cement, Alpena, Michigan.*

Steamer MERLE M. MCCURDY *at Great Northern Elevator, Buffalo, New York.*

Steamer J. B. FORD *at Huron Cement Company, Waukegan, Illinois.*

Steamer S. T. CRAPO, *Muskegon, Michigan.*

Steamer J. BURTON AYERS *arriving at South Chicago, Illinois.*

Steamer IRVIN L. CLYMER *approaching Milwaukee, Wisconsin.*

Steamer CRISPIN OGLEBAY, *Milwaukee, Wisconsin.*

Steamer CRISPIN OGLEBAY, *Milwaukee, Wisconsin.*

Steamer CRISPIN OGLEBAY, *Ashtabula, Ohio.*

Steamer JOHN G. MUNSON *arriving Conneaut, Ohio.*

Steamer S. T. CRAPO *departing Waukegan, Illinois.*

Steamer S. T. CRAPO *in Lake Michigan off Waukegan, Illinois.*